Hitchin'

A memoir
by Alex Silberman

Clink
Street

London | New York

Published by Clink Street Publishing 2019

Copyright © 2019

First edition.

ISBN:
978-1-913340-33-9 - paperback
978-1-913340-34-6 - ebook

Thanks to all of the characters I met along the way.

Special Thanks to Anthony, Nichole, Tom and Wendy for their help during the writing and editing process.

And of course The Ladies for all their support.

Chapter 1

6/23/15 Day 1 Tuesday

Quest:

A long or arduous search for something.

I walked down from Atlantic Ave. to the Boston Harbor and ceremonially dipped the toe of my right boot into the water of the Atlantic to begin my journey west. From the Boston Common, I strode toward the Public Gardens. Aside from the path, there were a few guys sitting on the dirt next to the grass. Their eyes caught the load on my back. We exchanged the basics.

"Where you goin?" they said looking interested.

I stopped and caught my breath. Sweat poured out of my body. The walk had caught up to me.

"Out to Santa Cruz," I said.

The outspoken one of the bunch who looked more tumble than rough spoke up.

"You know there's a lighthouse you should check out when you get out to Santa Cruz."

Then he mentioned a few other low cals. While he freely gave all this information, his tattered shirt hanging loosely. I couldn't help but think, 'Doubt I'm going to see any of the places he mentioned when I finally hit the left coast.' I left them with a cheery smirk motivated to get out of the city.

When I exited the city I took a detour to a private park overlooking a pond and had a piss. It started to sprinkle. I continued to walk anyway. The rain let up. By the time I reached the Highland green line station in Newton my clothes had more or less dried. I decided to climb over the railing and camp downhill from the tracks.

How does it feel to jack off in the bushes with two trains going by?

Adrenaline racing. Noise blurring, The wush of the train rushing by.

Body heightened until release.

Every muscle tightens. Rigid.

One brief moment gets obliterated.

Then everything softly floats back to earth

Rest by the green leaves and grass.

Along the fence, I and the synthetic sleeping bag lay there until morning's rude awakening.

I had made it out of the city to the start of Route 9 in Newton. Sunlight crept out of the overcast sky and the day's first light brought the chugging alarm of a locomotive.

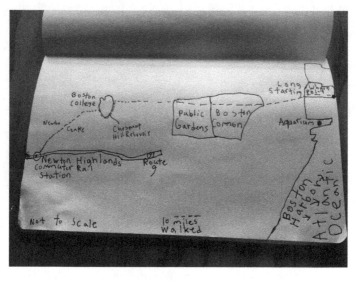

My quest started with wanting to walk from Boston to Santa Cruz, but after estimating how long that would take, hitching seemed the way to go. Why embark upon this journey in the first place? Could it be people were cast in grays so the choice remaining was movement or claustrophobia? Challenge, a rite of passage, or perhaps that indefinable drive when you imagine something and decide to put it into action. That visceral feeling that you must do it hungers at you each time you think about it. Words cease to define because the feeling is defined by the premonition of the action. And if that ain't a pretentious sentence I don't know what is.

***

Niagara Falls seemed fetching and a convenient way to enter Canada. The country to the north. I had never been. The Great Lake Michigan's crossing laid ahead. My sole planned luxury of the trip was the ferry ride across Michigan's water which seemed akin to the oceans' expanse along the coasts.

Ahh, Santa Cruz. Nostalgia for seventeen: learning to surf, walking the boardwalk, the end game of jumping into the Pacific from the Atlantic. All of it together was more than this. ALIVE!

6/24/15 Day 2 Wednesday

What's gonna happen? A prickling current in my arms rose up my neck to my head.

My thumb out. My feet stepped onward along the road. Head on a swivel. Eyes out for potential rides. My view for no one and everyone to open the road with their wheels.

Kenneth, the first and only ride of the day, took me north towards Framingham. A nice slim white guy wearing shorts and a well-worn t-shirt. He told me about traveling to New Zealand and how he hitched there while backpacking with his girlfriend. He's off to work at an organic veggie farm. Not much more than this brief experience was memorable about him. Traveling as a pair, let alone a couple, is no easy thing to do. At some point different interests and frustrations tend to arise. With Kenneth driving, I zoned out and thought of previous trips.

Past experience tells me that odd numbers work better, especially trios where the third can distract one of the first two when vitriol arises. When the relationship in the car is triangulated as opposed to two-sided, there is somewhere for built-up steam to go and dissipate. When disagreement happens, a third opinion can come in to sway the balance, leading into a decision or giving more gravity to one of the other two's thoughts. This is true whether it is a matter of greater or lesser significance. I have learned this from traveling with friends and family alike. And while it is true that the third party has the potential to make feelings and actions more heightened and egregious, from my experience, the former mediating effect has prevailed.

In past trips to Black Rock City, Nevada, from the Boston area and from Boston to Austin, the more positive result was proven out. The trio to Black Rock included me, an opinionated motivator edging us forward to our destination with my outdoor experience, James, formerly a tanker in Iraq, and young starry-eyed Cody, who at the start we thought of as just the younger brother of some mutual friends. At the time the three of us only knew each other in passing, but we all wanted to head to Burning Man for the first time. James clearly the best driver with steering wheel in hand nixed my abrasive music and Cody became the primary DJ. His favorite band also named James resonated out of the speakers. I would occasionally get into disagreements with James the tanker as the sun beat down on the Subaru heading west. Cody brought ease to these tensions with his positive, adventurous outlook on the trip and his light-hearted comments.

"Wow the sky looks sooo big!" he exclaimed as his eyes looked wide and upwards when we first made it out west.

In the trip to Austin, I took on the role of salve for the tensions in the vehicle. Our trio headed south, then west to Austin. Two members of the band Iqballers and I became their bullshit make-believe road manager. These two Iqballers were en route to meet up with the rest of the band in Texas. Peter the temperamental leader, Noah the idiosyncratic creative and I was the one keen for the adventure of the ride. I soon discovered my main job was making sure Peter did not kill or too unjustly verbally assassinate Noah before we got to Austin. I distracted, found music to listen to and tried to decrease tensions when he got bullish with his guilty victim. In the wee hours of a North Carolina morning, the cops pulled me over. Peter the leader got us out of trouble by playing it cool and we were back on the road posthaste. Noah to his credit funded most of the trip and rented the car in the first place. With three in the vehicle, both trips dysfunctionally functioned and everyone got where they wanted to go. Since the trips, I believe a two to one ratio is key to a successful long-haul road trip. Now as I pass by aimless gas stations and convenience stores with Kenneth I want to get where I want to go and play whatever role necessary to accomplish this objective. Even if it means temporarily subsuming my point of view.

I got out of the car near a green tract of land and wanted to cross over a pond, but there was no clear way on the road due to construction, so I headed down an access road to a trail to see if I could walk along a raised dam that had a building stuck in the middle, but it was a no go. I need an alternate route around the pond.

I went back to the trail. I passed a guy in his truck waiting for his work crew. I continued on the trail which led to train tracks that are parallel to the highway. I looped back around to continue toward central Mass. As the sun was starting to go down I rolled out my foam sleeping pad and set out the accompanying sleeping bag on top. Light, heat and mind ebb into restful darkness.

6/25/15 Day 3 Thursday – 6/29/15 Day 7 Monday

The trip was already three days old and I was frustrated to still be stuck in Massachusetts. Four rides under the belt, I arrived in Ware. The first of the day: a young guy trucking on his regular route.

"I got routes all over Central Mass," he said, his eyes lighting up as he went to the next delivery to drop his packages off.

I learned that he had done the festival circuit and seen a traveler or two. He pushed onward to the next destination and the momentum gave him kinetic energy.

We entered Worcester. The city seemed bright in the day's light despite its postindustrial depressed reputation.

"Thanks for the ride," I said as I hopped out at the light of a major intersection. My hopes were up and I readied myself to make a sign for Niagara.

I walked down the street and stopped off to use the facilities and refill water at the KFC. When I came out I spotted another delivery driver unloading his truck. I walked over and asked him, "Can you spare a large piece of cardboard?"

"Sure," he said, handing me the awkward and large floppy brown former box.

I took it over to the edge of the parking lot. Kneeling over the cardboard, I grabbed one of the large rounded black sharpies out of my black backpack and wrote out on the sign for the next destination west. I took my stretching rope out. So far it had only been used before nightfall or right after dawn to stretch my weary legs. My knife shone in the hot light of early summer as it poked two holes in the cardboard. The rope slid through each hole and I tied the ends together. I rigged my stretching rope and threw it over my neck to free my hands to display the sign.

I walked up the road to head out of Worcester. Some school kids walked towards me coming in the other direction. They chuckled and put out a hand each and I high-fived them. The youngest and smallest boy tried to put a Burger King crown on my head, but I wasn't having it. His eyes pleaded in amusement, my hand waved past him as I leaned my head away. I thought I'm not interested in his gift worthy of a pet.

Next, a guy who had hitchhiked decades ago picked me up and dropped me off in Brookfield. Back then he had been freed up. Since hitchin, he re-enrolled in the rat race albeit a more rural relaxed version than the city and was in town to pick up a car part.

In Brookfield, a young man made the next pickup.

"Thanks for the ride man," I said.

"Well you know I tried hitchhiking once and never got picked up. I waited out there for four hours and nothing."

"Well man, thanks for the ride. How far down Route 9 you headed?"

"A few miles down the road. I just got off work and now I'm heading home to see my wife."

As he dropped me off I got a warm feeling, and not just from the heat outside. It was about what he said about not getting picked up. Because of his own experience of not getting a ride, when he saw me on the side of the road, he decided to act with empathy. The type of empathy where you see yourself so clearly locked into the same challenging situation as another. Where you can feel the same hard road under your feet, the dusty bits of the road kicking up into your eyes as cars go whizzing past. When you're in the car and the man on the road is more akin than any driver in back or in front of you on that day. You have felt what he's feeling, walked as he's walking and longed for a path onward as he's longing. And for this reason, the bridge between me and the driver is clear as day.

Tip: Make a beeline to the bathroom trying not to raise too many eyes when passing through fast food establishments.

Chapter 2

Brandon Chaffee, what a ride! Who is this guy?

Standin' by Route 9 in a grass patch, sign flung over back attached to my stretching rope which hung over my neck. I took a drink of water.

(Mass accent) "Get the Fack in the Car!" A white pickup with a lot of shit in the back.

Hopped in, landing on shit.

"Keep ya head down so the cops don't see ya!" Going down the road thru town pulled off to a driveway in Ware. "What Where?"

"Hey, I'm Brandon look at my Donkey." He hops up, stands straight up, and poses on his donkey. "Oscar likes apples. Grab one."

"What r u a feisty kid or something?"

"No."

"What does your sign say?"

"Niagara Falls."

"You want a cocktail? I need a cocktail."

We hung out had a few drinks and smoked till it started to get dark and our stomachs began to rumble. We headed to a fine local restaurant for a delicious meal where Brandon knows the staff and I paid, with him promising, "I'll pay ya back real soon."

After the meal, we met one of the friendly waiters at the strip club back up the road. Brandon was getting along with the owner and talking about a possible event with poker and strippers on his land. Strippers performed in front of us. Brandon motioned to the more radiant one.

"Hey, do you wanna come with us? We're going to Niagara Falls tomorrow. I just met this guy today."

She said, "O I wish, but I just got in from Vegas and I gotta go and take care of my kid."

I fronted the money for much of the night's festivities which luckily Brandon paid back in full come morning. Didn't hurt that I got to crash out on a bed in his house.

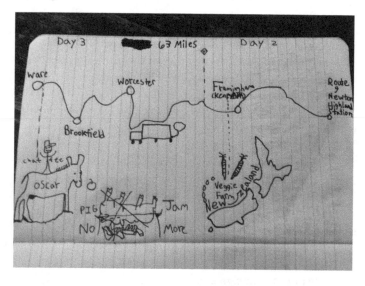

Off to Niagara we went the next day. So... there was a lot goin' on strife over a canceled festival, "Pig Jam" with mascot Oscar the Donkey, broken relationships abound girlfriend-wise, friend-wise, and lawsuit counterclaims because of issues with the festival property. Brandon going to town meetings calling people out for the amount of heroin moving through Ware.

Now off to the races with his voice in my head quotes of hilarity and advice:

God doesn't like a coward.

I'd look nice if I had a rich husband.

If you want something done ask someone that's already busy.

I got death threats in Worcester.

Passing outside Syracuse, heard about Dinosaur Bar-B-Que. Met two evangelists, one a bluesman at a gas station the other a Catholic toll taker. The toll taker spreading his word customarily out the window preaching the Catholic gospel. Both guys, along with Brandon, of course, had an extroverted self-confessional style embedded deep in American culture. The bluesman started to talk to me while Brandon was inside the gas station.

"I was drinking and deep into the blues. Now I've found the Lord and take care of my son." His eyes shone brightly with the infectious contagion he wished to infect us with.

Brandon walked out of the gas station towards us. Freshly purchased scratch tickets in hand, he enthusiastically dove into the conversation. He told the bluesman in quick succession, "Yeah well I'm trying to get the heroin out of my town and we're going to Niagara now." Pointing at me. "And I just met this guy the other day and now we're heading to the falls."

They went on for a bit, back and forth, then the bluesman wished us well and us him as he drove off in his black SUV. We pulled off on a side road and camped out between trees. Brandon's face lit up as we cooked meat over an open fire enthused at his first off-the-beaten-path camping experience. The night momentarily took hold. Few hours of sleep sun in the distance.

Misty to rainy coming into Niagara. The river sat alongside the car driving by, looking like it was not moving. Out on the precipice of rushing onward. The falls, my future, and Canada close by. Chemical-looking plants spotted the banks steam and smoke wafting out of them. They looked ready to spread their intoxicants to the dimly-lit river as if this was just as natural as the water flowing. Niagara has a few possible meanings. The most commonly accepted definition originates from the Iroquois word which means Strait, Onguiaahra. A narrow passage of water connecting two large bodies of water. But Niagara could also mean thundering waters, or it is also possible that Niagara was the name of a people who used to live by the river. In any regard, Chaffee and I would be by the heart of the river soon enough.

Arrived in Niagara parking lot at 6:33 am. After our eyes moved in and out of sleep for the next two hours we decided to hop on the boat *Maid of the Mist,* to see the falls and on this day the name proved prescient with more rain soon to come. Most of the other people on the boat were families. In fact, most of the people in general who walked the banks of Niagara in the daylight were either families or couples. The falls were impressive and the little girl in the Indian family next to us jumped up and down with excitement. Chaffee bellowed out even more enthusiastically. I was impressed with the mist and rain from the falls that came down on us. When the boat retreated from the falls though we turned to each other and I said, "Cool, well now what are we going to do?"

We were two grown guys and Niagara had a touristy Disneyland feel.

We walked out on the rainbow bridge to try to cross into Canada. Even though I knew that there was a good chance Chaffee might be blocked from getting in I thought it was worth a shot since he was so excited at a chance to leave the country for the first time. We walked along the bridge hopeful and asked the Canadian guard if it was possible to get in just for the day with a driver's license. He shook his head. With our spirits dampened we retreated. We told the American customs officer who let us back what happened and even he thought the Canadian Niagara was a hell of a lot better.

Chaffee was still excited to be in Niagara in spite of being disappointed that his not having a passport to Canada meant we had to stay on the American side. So we got a motel room on the edge of Niagara. Once in the room, he gets back with his girlfriend over the phone. (When I spoke to him a month later he said they had broken up again.)

I took him to his first casino and our funds went up and down with roulette. Got a tip from a Seneca guy about putting a smiley face on your sign when you're flying cardboard. Used one on each sign for the whole rest of the trip. For the time left in Niagara we hung out around town and at the motel, we gambled, and also found a homemade glow-in-the-dark mini-golf course. I decided to show Chaffee how to play American roulette. Chaffee and I sat at the table, the chips started coming in fast. What was once 200 was now 500. Chaffee started stacking them on multiple two to one payouts. I kept betting on black. We hit once, we hit twice. It kept going as we slowly accrued larger and larger stacks. The pit boss came over once, twice, seven times later. Another new dealer stood ready to spin the wheel as the pit boss peered over his shoulder. I pushed 100 on black. Red turned up. I pushed 200 on black.

Chaffee looked over eyes no longer filled with glee, "What are you doing?"

I simply said, "I gotta see."

Red turned. Fuck it I thought. Five hundred on black.

Chaffee said, "Really man what the fuck are you doing? We were doing so well."

"I gotta go for it."

We both stood up. The dealer spun the wheel. The pit boss's eye grew big. I turned my back as the ball rattled around. I turned back just as it found its home. Click click.

Red. Chaffee looked down. I stood up and as I walked away said, "Sometimes you just gotta go for it."

I figured out right after they hustle ya that so no one pays off a dealer, dealers are switched multiple times in and out.

After the loss, I bid farewell to Chaffee and crossed the rainbow bridge for the second time. Now, alone and with a passport, I made it across the bridge and customs was a different story.

I reflected on the past days as I waited in customs. As time went by, Chaffee's shoulders had loosened, the sharp frenzied look in his eyes abated and he was no longer swimming like a shark in a small aquarium, I talked calmly with him and focused his energy steadily on what was to come. He got a pig spirit animal figurine at a stand outside of where we had played indoor glow-in-the-dark mini golf, it said, "The determination to take the right actions in your life." The pig bonded and grounded him back to his festival.

To this day we are still bandying about with an idea for a show called "Pimp Your Hitchhiker." It would be similar to "Pimp my Ride by Xzibit." ("Hitch your Pimp" would be even more challenging.) We would travel around the country by car and pick up hitchhikers and bring them to their destination, but first, show them a night out on the town and other goodies like Brandon Chaffee did for me. When he took me in, he shared his vision of Pig Jam taking me on a tour of his land. Pig Jam was a small festival where there was music and he would put a large pig on a spit and cook for everyone. That's why Pig was his spirit animal.

His form clearly jumps to mind, eyes always looking mind a hive of activity and emotionality. His bald head with a cap propped up on top, long jean shorts with a t-shirt he had clearly been sweating in and work boots. His body a working man's with a bit of a belly past thirty years.

We went off-roading up a trail in back of his house with his truck as he knocked off his rearview mirror on a tree trying to squeeze through the gap in the woods. We duct-taped it back on the next day when we got to Northampton. Chaffee was always sharing his drinks, food, ideas, and opinions. One of the most giving guys I've met. I think I'll see him soon.

Tip: Put a smiley face on your sign when you're flying it. This has the potential to consciously or subconsciously affect drivers positively and they'll be more likely to pick you up.

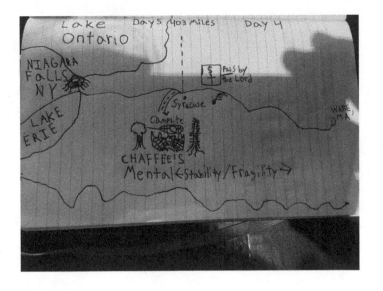

Chapter 3

Customs was concerned about my entrance into the Great White North. I waited two hours with the rest of humanity in the generic government building. It wasn't long, but it was a bland purgatory similar to the RMV. Finally I got up to the booth.

"How long will you be spending in Canada?"

"A few days to a couple weeks"

"Where are you going?"

"Through Ontario to Michigan."

"Do you have a bus ticket?"

"No."

Eyebrows raised, "Well are you staying with anyone in Canada?"

"No, I'm planning on hitching across." His eyes grew wider, brow furrowed and a look of concern played across his face as a pink hue came lightly through his cheeks.

"Well, most people come over just for the day."

"Yeah well, I'm planning on heading straight thru."

"How much money do you have on you?"

"I have a couple hundred in cash and I'm going to exchange it straight away."

With a look of mothering concern, he stamped my passport and I was thru.

I finally relaxed once I was safe across the street now officially in Canadian Niagara. It already looked better than the American side. Tacky colorful Disney mascotted stores were out on one of the main side streets. The expansive park with walking paths was the real attraction. It helped that the day before it had been raining in American Niagara and now in Canadian Niagara, it was sunny and green. Canadian Niagara simply held a larger population and a friendlier feeling. The park a long swath of bright green grass. The American Niagara was a more depressing gray, pushier, it was simply less and I had lost money there.

I immediately went to the casino to gamble, to win back the money and reserve tickets for Canada Day. The Casino Niagara was a little sleepier and easily more profitable than the one on the American side. I tapped on the window of a car. It was a Daniel Cape doppelganger. Daniel Cape was a director of a summer camp I worked at in Ukraine. He gave me a ride to a creek and proceeded to mow the lawn on the bank which made a good place to sleep. He even gave me bug spray for the winged menaces of the night. Both men had glasses and were of similar average stature with a kind way about them.

I watched the sun go down as a few boats sleuthed up and down the creek. Happened upon some muddied porn mags as the summer mosquitos lazily drifted out making themselves known.

6/30/15 Day 9 Tuesday

Breakfast at the casino, walked there from the creek passing by what looked like the industrial side of something similar to a Canadian sea world. After the meal, a view from the other side looked pleasing. Cops pull me off a ledge overlooking the falls as I am sketching a picture of some of the rapids. Smart move! Guy grabbed me by the back of the shirt, think I was more likely to slip in reaction. Showed them the picture that I had made and told them that was all that I was doing while they ran my passport and warned me that it was a popular place for jumpers. Quite a parks department they got. Went to Harvey's for poutine, that oh so heavy Canadian fast food. Fries with cheese curds and gravy smothering it with a bit of bacon added in for flavor. A fine way to go into cardiac arrest and had it been winter not summer as good a way as any to warm up with minimal movement. Summer made poutine into a gut bomb and I began to sweat the second I stepped outside.

7/1/15 Day 10 Wednesday

Light shone through the pines. Something creeping rubbed on the zipper of the sleeping bag. Eyes still glossed over. The light shifted something green into focus. First one then another all rising from the dried brown pine needles. Just little sprigs. They looked all the same though even with their three bright leaves they were not visible by night. The itch grew again and rubbing my wrist was of no help. Bringing the back of my hand to my face O I knew now what I had done. Seeing all of this poison ivy around me I growled and rose. I focused on grabbing a dead leaf and surgically uprooted the sprigs of poison shielded in leaves and pinched them between my thumb and forefinger before casting them away from the pines. Only after I had done a once-over of the pine needle bed did I get out the meager first aid kit and apply anti-itch salve and bandages to the newly infected wrist. Once the wrist was wrapped, onward and outward, away for the time being.

Canada Day. Went to see a combination of performers from *The Voice* and *American Idol*, definitely a surreal experience with fireworks going off over the falls just as I exited the casino. Not much gambling while I had been waiting to see the show. Taking the risk to gamble money seems akin to the traveling spirit. I was already out there gambling with rides not knowing who would pick me up, if anyone would pick me up at all, or where I would lay my head for the night. When you're already taking one risk adding a different calculated risk tends to be easier to slip into. The thing I like about casinos, similar to McDonald's, is that they tend to have a darker sense of utilitarianism. Almost anyone is let in. Being American with hidden taxes on everything from a soda initially priced at $1.99 ending up be being $2.11 at the register to random daily fees, a casino tends to rip the veneer off capitalism. Put your money down, you know the odds are stacked against you in the house's favor, but at least you know their odds. As much hustle as they are, there is actually a chance you could win a chunk of money. Whereas the American delusion of get rich quick schemes and the myth telling you that *you can be rich too if you just work hard* sells you a bill of goods. Believe that and you might as well be floating in a boat towards the falls without a paddle.

To get back the money on the Canadian side I slowly stacked up chips only to start going on a losing streak after doubling down successively. I was keeping careful track of how many chips I had. There were a couple psychological advantages I had compared to gambling on the American side. For one, Canadians are less pushy and let you take your time deciding. People came in and out, but for the most part, it was just me and the man with the silver ball. It was daytime and I was in no rush. Still, my chips were running down and I just took the risk taking a tall stack of nickels and betting them on the outside. The risk paid out. I then small bet my way up with $5, $10, or $20 dollar bets back up to over $500. Then I made what is always the most important decision: to cash out and leave.

Coming out into the night lights the street that sloped down to the falls glowed. People milled about excitedly, moving to and fro. Booms from the river red and white flashed in lines toward the stars, the air fresh and wet. My eyes were still readjusting from the performance and inside fluorescent light. Bleariness stunned by the contrast of frivolity outdoors. A few more thunders of smoke inducing light.

It was not the Fourth of July it was not as big and happening as Boston.

There I stood and walked to better vantage points. Past ten o'clock in Niagara, Ontario, Canada, so familiar yet so different from the land across the river. I imagined past July's merging into the present, thinking how there had been no war for independence here and maybe this made the people different from their more violent and independent American neighbors.

7/2/15 Day 10 Thursday

Walked out of Niagara. I met another guy out wandering. He had just exited a KOA campground. He said, "It was good there I made a whole bunch of campfires." He had a shaved head and this big leather military style duffle backpack. I gave him 5CDs because he looked like he could use it. He smoked me up getting me lightly stoned for the walk ahead. He was headed to a homeless shelter 13km west. He wanted to rest and I wanted to go on.

Had the shortest pick up of the whole trip at 1km to a gas station. Next, I imposed a lift from a driver, who had just stopped to talk on the phone. He had not stopped to pick up anyone walking down the road. He swore to himself that he would never give another hitchhiker a ride after another one years ago had shown him the big knife he used for protection.

His daughter though got around the ski slopes in Alberta where she lives by hitching. He told me I could have a handful of farm fresh cherries as I went out on the road. Sweet both in taste and act.

I walked for a while, it was hot as hell but not quite as hot as it would be in northwest Utah.

Going down a rural road near a farm two guys called over, "You want a Bud?"

Normally I'd tell them to go to hell in different words for their beverage choice.

"Sure man," I said while thinking fucking disgusting on multiple levels, chemical rice water with alcohol thrown in. Beer for someone who doesn't want the taste of real beer, just shitty intoxication. But damn it was good cold on that day. The guys brought me back to the shed to hit a lung-wrenching bong. Normal questions about the trip and general friendliness, nothing too specific in conversation, with a bong helping to wipe the memory. Then they drove me to a junction of the interprovince and left me with some wine cigars, black, mild, and thin with the plastic mouthpiece on the end. Stopped in for a 10CD meal at a bar and the owner saw my stuff and said that I could camp out on a nice patch of grass in back. Perfect another friendly Canadian had already given me the tenner earlier in the day thinking with my sign I was heading home to Michigan. I crashed out immediately.

Tip: If you run into a nervous or suspicious driver, for the first little while of the ride, you may want to treat um like a cop. Keep your hands where they can see them. No sudden movements. Topical conversation may relax them and this edict will hopefully become unnecessary after a spell.

Tip: If you choose to carry a knife keep it hidden unless there is a good reason for bringing it out.

Chapter 4

7/3/15 Day 11 Friday

Started heading down the road and eventually when I had taken a turn to get on the more major highway a Canadian policeman pulled over and told me that I needed to exit off for my own safety.

"There's dangerous drivers on these roads."

The Canadian police were cute compared to their counterparts in the land of the Me and home of the slave. More maternalistic in nature like the nanny state whose queen was still on their money. Playing in my head, in a British accent, *it's for your own good darling.*

Anyway ended up walking by a strawberry seller and a car that had passed me by earlier heading the other way now stopped and rolled down the window. Woman by the name of Mary-Anne asked if I needed a ride. Strange, nicer neighborhood, a bunch of golf courses around, and the first ride from a woman on the trip. She took me back to her place and I met her husband and her adult kids. Took a shower, she threw my dirty clothes in the laundry and I changed into pants and a shirt of her husband Donny. Still have the shirt that says "I got Lucky at the Brassie." Had a delicious steak dinner with corn, a full family meal. Then we played cornhole out in the yard with the sun setting over the crops. One board stars and stripes, the other a Maple Leaf. Mary-Anne showed me her garden with squash, beans, and maize planted symbiotically together named the Iroquois Three Sisters as well as the many edible and healing plants. She repeatedly advised me as to what was useful and grew wild in the area. We sat around drinking beers and their friends who trained dogs came over. Donnie bumped music on high-quality speakers in the backyard and showed me his whole music promotions business and studio in the garage. Megan their daughter left to go hang out with her boyfriend. The rest of us had delicious watermelon for dessert mowing down on it in the kitchen and to top it off, I got to crash out in the trailer parked in front of the house. Talk about hospitality.

7/4/15 Day 12 Saturday

Morning, we ate at the local diner with everyone from the night before, friends and family included, and then they dropped me at the roadside to hitch along once again. That night I ended up sleeping near the on-ramp on the edge of London looking to head towards Sarnia.

Mary-Ann Megan Donny

7/5/15 Day 13 Sunday

Ride from a Delaware First Nation woman from London to Sarnia who was used to picking up hitchhikers. The pedestrian crossing from Sarnia to Port Huron was no more so I got a ride from Jon, a bridge-playing bachelor in his 70s with a liking for history from the Canadian point of view. Jon had run into the same challenge of trying to cross by foot previously. He told of the War of 1812 and detailed the relationship of the Ontario, Michigan border.

"There's a big float celebration each year with boats and tubes that drives border patrol on each side crazy as no one cares if they float to one side or the other. Authorities have learned to somewhat look the other way during the celebration."

He drove me down to the Sombra Ferry and I crossed back into the USA full of Tim Horton's he bought me. Any time in Canada and you learn this all-purpose fast food store is just as ubiquitous as McDonald's is south of the border.

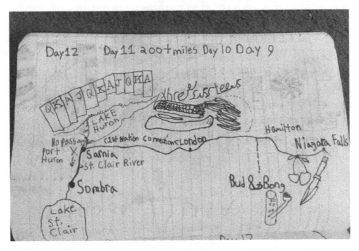

Most rides in a day, six total four on the U.S. side. The first upon arriving from Sombra to Marine City Michigan was a cop. She had mistaken me for a guy who currently had a warrant out for his arrest. He was obviously on the run. I had just started to walk down the long hot 26 Mile Road leading west. I was coming out from a nearby gas station where a nice couple drove by and gave me cold refreshing Powerades. Once the cop pulled me over she waited for backup. I was back in America and my illusions of Michigan did not disappoint. After running the license and hearing the fugitive had been spotted elsewhere she gave me a ride to the end of her jurisdiction on 26 Mile Road and told me about her family trips to the Upper Peninsula. "It looks like another world."

The only unnerving thing along the ride was looking at the doors and realizing there was no way I could unlock them on my own.

Then a weed-smoking veteran came along when I thought I was in hitchhiker hell. The formula is as follows: Prison + Golf Course = No Pickup, Michigan Correctional Facility to be precise. On the 69 ramp a middle finger from a passing car brought a smirk to my face. The sign I was holding had two smiley faces with tongues out upside down to each other. Then rollin' up quick a high energy guy in a sports car that was all about the random. Slicked back hair, he and his wife back home were caretakers for the disabled. Final ride of the day from Imlay City through Flint he stopped at the hardware store to look for a chainsaw piece and then we drove to Lansing. Quite a juxtaposition from the cop. Shades on, slight, he was going to pick up his hooker friend to drop her off for a date. She was feeling a bit dope sick and he had a wife that still would not divorce him. He met the hooker when he was flying a sign on the street. Dropped me off and I night walked to a better on-ramp for pickups in Lansing. It was magical with tons of light bugs illuminating the way.

Tip: If you're riding with a junkie make sure they stay awake with their hands on the steering wheel and stay generally in their own lane. Nodding out can be fatal.

Chapter 5

7/6/15 Day 14 Monday

Guy possibly gay with a shaved bald head and goatee picked me up after sleeping in a parking lot near the on-ramp and dropped me off in Grand Rapids. I thought he might be hitting on me as he patted on his leg with his right hand, but I just changed the subject to what he might want to do in the future. He started as an awkward guy but by the end of the ride after talking about potential travel jobs like teaching English in Southeast Asia he turned out to be nice enough. It's a struggle not to judge people, and at the same time to not put myself in a bind.

Stopped for lunch at a supermarket. Called fam and heard back from Chaffee that he had bought land off of I-90 in New York where we previously had seen deer, I was glad to hear for the moment all was well with his girl. The realtor for his land in Mass just arrived to discuss selling his former festival plot. NY 80 acres cost 90K which he had put down a deposit on. Started walking and the first couple of the trip gave me a ride to the better on-ramp of I-96 to Muskegon. Got door-to-door service from a couple of guys, one in IT, the passenger helping him work, a former small-time heroin transporter and also a user. He used to take the train to Chicago with his girlfriend at the time, and they would look like a nice white couple unsuspicious to authorities. Their dealer would put them in a hotel in the city and break them off a piece for personal use before they headed back up north.

Tip: When you get into a vehicle keep em talking, they may take you farther than originally thought.

Tip: When you get into someone's car for the first time all they can see is the person in front of them. They know not your story nor you theirs. Both of you will have to hazard guesses for your own protection and well-being. All either of you can judge before words are uttered is simply what your senses can take in. Try to find objectivity. You might have more in common than you thought.

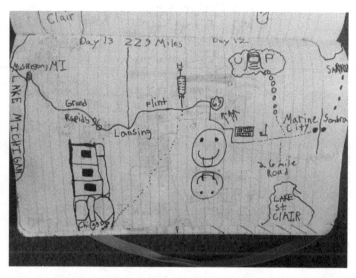

Chapter 6

The ferry from Muskegon to Milwaukee was named Lake Express. Riding the ferry to Milwaukee looks like crossing the ocean. I happened to meet an older biker from San Diego who in his last bit did nineteen states and 9,000 miles.

Walked across Milwaukee and slept underneath an overpass for I-94. It was pouring and I had gotten soaked trying to set up camp underneath a tree in a small park so the bridge would have to do. Although loud underneath I-94 it had a flat landing in between the underside of the bridge and the steep ramp that comes up from the sidewalk. Restless slumber.

7/7/15 Day 15 Tuesday

Went to a convenience store owned by an Indian family, got a better map of Wisconsin and made a sign for Madison. Called cousin Susan who lives there and let her know I might be there today or tomorrow. Arrived in Madison and went up to the capital building, called her. She said to call her back at 8pm. Beforehand hung out in the park with four junkies nearby overlooking one of the lakes. Went to a cafe ordered a Mexican hot chocolate and read *Smithsonian* magazine. Chaffee called in, and I was now running late to meet Susan. Met her and went through family photos of Bernstiens who are on my biological mother's side. There were a few I remembered, but most of them were more my mother or grandparent's generation. I stared at them with a vague look of recognition as she explained how everyone was related. Met her husband who had just gotten the complete collection of *The Decline of Western Civilization*. They both had glasses well-focused eyes and shorter hair. Their eyes held long memories from reading, digesting, formulating, and making presentations to students. Eyes used to communicate understandings. I was focused on the baseline at the time. Eat almonds, sorbet, drink beer. More conversation... Susan joked that she would quiz me on family history and people's names and who they were related to in the morning... sleepover.

   Tip: Family and friends are a comfort on the road. They are also the most likely to throw you off the way you would have things done. Their concerns are valid. Their concerns are valid for them. They are not your concerns.

Chapter 7

7/8/15 Day 16 Wednesday

Wake up talk to Susan have breakfast briefly and went over the family photos and was quizzed with mixed results. Susan made sure to correct any mistakes. Eat pizza with her husband who is a few years younger than her and talked about "life n hitchin as a Lost Art." Lost Art as if the heyday of hitching was decades past when there was a more willing common cultural sensibility. Susan and her husband are both professors at the University of Wisconsin They are especially concerned as they are parents so they project their own daughter Flora, an only child, onto me as if she was the one traveling and facing dangers. Her husband helped drop me off at RT 18/151.

Fastest pickups of the trip after walking out of Madison. Buddhist yoga young woman dressed in full monk attire and shaved bald head as a teacher she intended to take students to India as the climax of their learnings. Older guy late 60s to 70s musician who played "Wagon Wheel" the night before. Smoked weed with a woman who is a chef and husband worked at the "Montchevre" goat cheese plant. She wanted to go to Dubuque but couldn't find her credit card. The last couple of the day, guy a motormouth with a cowboy hat and they were looking for weed. Said he used to work for NASA and is an atheist. Got dropped off in Dubuque and started walking out. Campcd on a hill next to a farm under a pine tree.

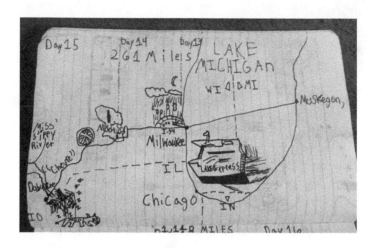

7/9/15-7/10/15 Days 17-18 Thursday-Friday

Goin across Nebraska listening to country. Picked up yesterday by Caitlyn, a grandmother in a white Chrysler convertible. We then spent the night in a motel in Iowa friendly to pets. The room had two beds and we took turns going in and out of the bathroom. I rolled on over to the side facing away from her and got some shuteye. The next day we headed toward Colorado. We pass by a truck of half green tires. Caitlyn tells me all about her life.

"I taught young children, I've been married, I've had kids and now grandkids. And when you're involved in a marriage, I believe people give up too easily. I think that if you're going to end a relationship especially a marriage you should really make sure the other person is ok and that they have enough time to grieve."

"Really?" I said.

"Yes, you should always end a relationship with someone else's feelings in mind. I was in a relationship with a man I met on a study retreat. And he really loved me. He was a reverend.

I told him I had kids. He seemed fine with it. But when he did finally move in he only stayed three months. He really loved me, but he just couldn't deal with living with me and the kids. The house was fun but chaotic. I still loved him. His leaving really hurt though."

She looked wistful, seemingly remembering how she formed her opinions of how things should be. She continued, "I would see my parents in the living room. All of us kids were supposed to be asleep. They always made sure they had their adult time. We would sneak down and look through the railing at them sitting together. I always remembered that's how it should be."

Now she was driving west coming on down from her life in Duluth. She said, "I never really thought about it before, but my daughter, who now has a daughter of her own who is just as challenging as she was, asked about grandma going on this trip. My daughter replied, 'Your grandma's a free spirit.'"

Caitlyn paused for a moment to think about it, and said, "I guess I am."

We headed into the state that means red in Spanish though now it was turning green fast. The law had recently changed to the DEA's dismay and so it was attracting alternative tourists and those seeking more natural medicine. As well as being the most in shape Colorado also has the most skin cancer from the elevated heights its citizens take up the Rockies. Soon after we crossed the border we spotted a tourist information center. We went in and found out about the nearest body of water that was ripe for cooling the body on this hot summer day.

At a lake park in eastern Colorado, we cooled off and revived the senses. Ready to get back on the highway, but which way was the highway? The man who gave us directions back to the interstate was a man in the smallest town ever, he sounded and had mannerisms that looked like a wind-up doll. Similar to Woody from *Toy Story*. As if a string was pulled out from his back and he only had time for a slow drawl of words to come out before the string went back into his spine and the string would have to be pulled again for another response.

Idaho Springs, CO, Mountain Time. The tub in the room on the second floor was a two-person jacuzzi with a small river running in the back of the Argo Suites. The Argo Suites hotel seemed to have the last decent room in town. Caitlyn called her ex as she had done previously and he shelled out money for the room. The town was a mountain rustic tourist enclave with shops and bars spotted along the one main street.

I ended up going to the pizza place called Picci's, recommended by the affable young gay man at the front desk. Great place with the cook who made our custom pizza and Big Mama Rina who helmed the register and poured everybody in the joint shots as she talked up a storm. She had a motorcycle out front and her name came from being the mother to two big ole boys who were now grown men. A brief flash of sadness slackened her face when she said,

"My boys have moved away."

Then she brightened again. Her attitude somewhere between mountain woman and straight-up New York not that she was from there. I could have easily mistaken her for that tough New York Italian mother, making sure everyone had enough and a good time to boot as well as keeping everyone in line as she kept wisecracking and taking orders, round body moving around from the register with her big bosoms leading the way. She walked outside and showed everyone her hog that seemed to sparkle even in the dark. The red paint gleamed off the center of her bike and we hugged her goodbye.

I split off from Caitlyn as she stayed at the hotel and I went out to the bar where we had stopped in before to ask about a place to stay. Caitlyn had remarked on the rugged beauty of the women when we first entered the town. The bartending western women you can see how they catch a man's mind. The bartender definitely fit the bill with capable hands which moved quickly over the pints and long hair and cutoffs. It would be no surprise to see a greasy wrench in her hand instead of the glasses she wielded deftly from behind the taps. The energy though came from another part of the room.

Gal thought I was a fellow doppelganger raft guide she had messed around with in the past. She came up repeatedly to hug me saying the last time, "I hope you don't hate me." Finally, after she wouldn't believe I wasn't the man in question, I said, "I don't hate you."

A drunken smile spread over her face as I strode away. In the dim light on the near side of the room sat the only dog allowed into the bar. I sat down next to the dog's owner. He told me he supported the women's competitive raft trip to Brazil and his dog had become a special mascot of the women's team. With the guides and western bar feel, it felt Prescott Outdoors familiar. This was the town of my college where I had lived for four years of my life. I came back to the hotel a few drinks in and although Caitlyn had invited me to share the huge bed she had something like a really bad case of eczema on her legs that put me off. Though physically it would not have infected me I was better off rolling my mat out once again this time on the small deck overlooking the rushing creek that streamed behind the hotel.

7/11/15 Day 19 Saturday

After seeing a man in the morning panning the creek for gold and hitting the Safeway for supplies Caitlyn dropped me off in West Vail. I imagined the area's steep green mountain passes covered in powder ready to traverse like a Warren Miller movie. Rides: one pizza delivery guy, high school teacher talked about stoned kids and geology, rock climbing construction worker driving a Hummer. Started raining on the drive to Slit. Young couple with a pit mix and breathalyzer attached to the ignition now common from experience in the southwest. Motorbiker from Aspen smoked a bowl exchanged stories and knew about *Thumbs Up*. *Thumbs Up*, an inspiring YouTube hitchhiking show with a hardy goofy sense of humor. Dave Cho the famed graffiti artist now well known in the public eye unfortunately for his Facebook stock goes with his buddy though it is completely unclear how they are related throughout the series. He gives tips along the way about how to travel, like how do you negotiate things when you don't speak a word of the language. He also does interviews with all sorts of humanity they come across from the kindest giving folks to downright racists. It enthralled me and showed me concretely that this way of moving across the land could be done undeterred. From planes, trains, and automobiles, to river rafting on an inflatable mattress and bypassing international borders.

Back to reality, a couple going to Moab picked me up in a two-car caravan as the water was waning and they told me they built straw bale houses then they dropped me at Grand Junction. The young guy selling peaches near the gas station gave me one and I got the last two hot dogs from the convenience store cashier. Camped out across from the airport.

Tip: If you haven't hitched or traveled in nontraditional transport the vice YouTube series *Thumbs Up* is a good place to start.

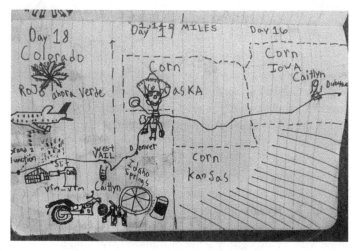

Chapter 8

7/12/15 Day 20 Sunday

Identification: A person's association with or assumption of the qualities, characteristics, or views of another person or group.

Where do I stand with who I am in this world? Where do you stand? What is one's interpretation of one's self?

Explosive expert first pickup to Fruita. In Fruita, picked up by Michael a former hitchhiker and truck driver with a new 2014 "Bracha" company truck. He told me of how he used to hitch and gave me $10 telling me to save it for a beer upon arriving in Santa Cruz and call him when I arrived. He would wipe his face every so often just to keep himself awake along the long stretch of empty western road. Drove to the junction of I-15 and I-70W.

Rob picked me up he's a construction worker doing tiles which has him traveling all over. Paraphrased "Have six stepkids two biological. I used to hitchhike and I got a few stories. When I was hitching a cop picked me up as I was waiting by the side of the road."

"What are you doing?"

"Bullshitting, I was doing a college paper researching the decline of the American Hobo from the 60's to the present. He was surprised, interested and wanted to know more. So I told him all about it. The cop kindly picked up his bag full of unbeknownst weed and placed it down gently beside me as he left me by the side of the road."

Strange that both Rob and I had gotten amiable rides that brought us closer to our destinations by cops.

Rob rambled on, "Again by the roadside a bit closer to the Mexican border, this time border patrol rolls up. Decked out in their green oh so serious uniforms the young Chicano border patrol points to me then to the vehicle and they open it on up. I get into the vehicle and they take me back to the station giving me a sandwich in holding. When I got called up to be processed they start talking to me in Spanish. I talked back to them in English and they tell me my English is way too good."

"Where ya from?"

"Dallas Fort Worth."

"Then why the hell did you get in the car?"

"Well I was hitchhiking you told me to get in. Border patrol was stunned ended up giving me a total of three sandwiches and sent me on my way."

Rob mentioning offhand as he glanced at the dusty desert going by, "Speaking of Dallas Fort Worth I used to run the rave scene there supplying all the acid and ended up skipping town when law enforcement was closing in. My lawyer later told me that I could have been charged with terrorism because the government was saying that you could use the volume of acid as a mind control device by slipping it into the local water supply." Rob's right hand drifted down to the bottom of the wheel as he seemed to grow comically nostalgic for the crazy old days.

"Another time a native guy who picked me up dropped me at his sister's place saying I could stay there. The sister comes out asking, "Who are you? Sayin she's pissed. My brother just took my weed and left."

"Well I think we can work something out," Rob said with a smile. "Ended up working on the rez for a lil while thereafter."

The last of the stories was a young man's fantasy. "Cougar picks me up drives me back to her big ole house in California her little plaything gets mad seeing another man, she kicks him out. Proceeds to fuck my brains out, For real!"

Rob also talked about his ex-wife and her new husband. His mood had changed from his other stories to agitated. He gripped the steering wheel tighter and his eyes flicked back and forth over the scenery in front of him.

"I went to my daughter's birthday party and stayed as long as I could stand it. I got to hear it from my ex-wife." His animus grew as his eyes became dead focused on the road ahead. "I stayed as long as I could for my daughter's sake."

His goatee now greying, left hand higher on the wheel at eleven, right hand down at four, somewhere in his forties I guessed. He said, "I'm planning to move my whole family to Nevada so I can be closer to my daughter I'll get a house down the street I'm sure my ex-wife will love that!"

I looked out the window, the highway seemed to go infinitely into the open sparse Utah desert. The mood was lighter once again as the stoning had done its work on both of us.

Dropped off by Rob in Provo. I walked to the next exit. Picked up by a mother originally from PA and her three kids ten and under. Three-year-old vomited as I got out in Lehigh. Mormon couple out for a drive playing Black Sabbath. They have older kids staying back at home. Listening to metal was a thing they did commonly after church, their Sunday tradition. She was originally from Detroit and reminded me of fond memories of Michigan. They dropped me off outside of Salt Lake and I crashed out for the night.

7/13/15 Day 21 Monday

The nice enough metal Mormon couple dropped me off, but damn if hitching out of Salt Lake was not panning out. Military grade trucks passed by. A few cars passed by, but there was no passage towards the barren west of northern Utah. It could be the hot death and nothingness out this way. It could be the buttoned-up small office buildings and hotel on the way to the on-ramp. It could be that Salt Lake was plain in the opposite direction. For whatever the reason though the fact of the matter was the day grew hotter and I still did not have a ride.

I started walking down old I-80 west in heat. Sat down as sweat came across my brow. The sweat didn't stay long as the desert sun dried it. Rest, just for a few minutes, a moment, ten minutes. Hips need grease like gears to keep turning. Student truck drivers drove by.

A pickup truck pulled alongside. Looked up into the sun towards him. The driver tells me he used to hop the engine room car on trains. He picks me up in his pickup truck and gives me a ride to the Flying T Truckstop. Meet three other hitchhikers two guys and a gal. She's eighteen, Asian, blonde with dreadlocks, slim and androgynously dressed in flannel. She has already been train-hopping for six months. Both the guys have been traveling for years and the face and arms of the one in overalls are covered in soot and dirt, alongside him sits his loyal pit mutt. He has a sign that says, "Fat guy likes chicken." The girl is trying to head to some train-hopper meetup in Nevada. Of the four of us, she's getting the antsiest as there are no rides heading west.

I bumped into the traveler without the dog washing hands in the Flying T. Says he's wondering where she went. 'Must a got bothered by the guys and took off.' Still, no rides heading west. I say fuck it, say bye to the guys and start walking into the desert towards Grantsville the next town over. The cargo trains on the edge of humanity in Utah were Union Pacific. Walk along an access road to the train tracks. It leads to a hole underneath the raised-up track and in the distance, I get to see the Salt Lake as the sun sets. Continue walking on the tracks until crashing near a fence after sixteen miles.

Tip: There are class levels and cliques on the street just like in any other part of society

Tip: The sun can be brutal and drain your limited resources quickly. If choosing to walk a long distance in the desert wait until the sun starts to go down. The night is your friend. Many more miles can be covered then. You can sleep when you find a relatively safe spot come morning.

Tip: Wear proper attire. Similar to going on a camping trip. Synthetic materials and wool work well. Your feet are key. Make sure they are adequately maintained. Of any part of your body, your feet are the most likely to get beat up day after day. If you are dropped in the middle of nowhere and no cars are around, your feet can be your only lifeline out.

Chapter 9

7/14/15 Day 22 Tuesday

Morning…

Saw an exit for town hop the barbed wire fence. Walked to Grantsville. Got reminded by a store cashier about the casino shuttle to Wendover the furthest west reach of Utah. Got a ride while walking back to the TA truck stop from a daughter and mother.

Waiting for an $11 casino shuttle and I'm frustrated, but looking to get the fuck out of Utah. I had been stuck in this desert purgatory far too long. The day before the other hitchhiker had said: "Utah where compassion comes to die. They think the church does all the work so they don't have to." He started traveling at sixteen and was now in his thirties full of experience. The last bit about the church brought to mind the New York rapper Immortal Technique. "This ain't a Christian Nation mothafucka please America never taught me to turn the other cheek."

$1 from a family with a Nevada plate same place as the sign I was holding.

6 pm

As I'm waiting for the shuttle at 6:30 I see a young native guy with a backward baseball cap and green shirt flying a sign. So many hitchhikers have been here before. Go over give him a buck. And start walking back toward TA. A black Dodge Ram pulls up. And the train-hopping hitchhiker I had met a day

before pops out and says, "If you want a ride talk to the driver."
I do and the young guy with a baseball cap hops in the van.
The train-hopper had managed to cut his companion loose.
Driver by the name of Kyle wants weed I say my friend Jon is in
SAC and I call him and he says he has three grams of hash. He
says we can drop in. Kyle is a hippieish looking big dude with
dyed bleach blond hair and bare feet. The fourth member of
the van is a seventeen-year-old street punk with a high opinion
of himself. He thinks of himself as being very good looking.
His name is Johnny. The native kid is twenty, an artist with
a thick sketchbook and his name is Isiah. Everyone showers
except me. The guys have been quickly hopping in and out of
a timed shower that runs off quarters and I don't want to have
the shower stop mid-rinse or be left behind. Also, I just want
to get on the road and away from the truck stop after waiting
for so long.

As we take off, a version of a classic folk punk traveler tune
comes to mind. "This car is a war machine it runs on nicotine
and gasoline said we gotta go go go driving on the wrong side
of the road. This car is a war machine it runs on blood and
gasoline." It's by Johnny Hobo and The Freight Trains, a well-
known folk punk band among travelers and maladjusts.

TA truck stop to Wendover we stopped at the Salt Lake
which was really a salt flat. We get a taste and see the yoga girls
in black tights posing as the sun goes down for a "calendar
shoot." Kyle broke down about his girl, guys comfort him.
Yoginas gymnastically body balance as punk boys look on n
holler out. We headed off towards Wendover. Park and I split
off to gamble. $35 cash back from two casinos. Threw all down
to the guys and had a rock stacking competition with Johnny
who had a seventeen-year-old light in his eyes and dyed 'hawk.
There was talk to gas station customers trying to get weed.
Train-hopper's pit jumped ten feet up in the air trying to climb
up the convenience store wall and came right down where he
started. The dog had learned orders well and knew to "load
up" when his owner gave the command to get in a car or train.

Ended up setting an example for the punk boys' young pit and their dog imitated the older pit loading up on command. Stayed out lost $400 on roulette and slots. At Mickey D's Isiah told me his girl back home was six months pregnant. To him, this was his last big adventure before taking full responsibility as a father. The end of his freewheeling teenage lifestyle was near and adulthood was going to arrive with a solid jolt, though not just yet. The heaviness of the moment would have set in more had life not been moving so fast. The mood was nothing that was about to happen was relevant until it was there happening in your face and you had to act and react in the present.

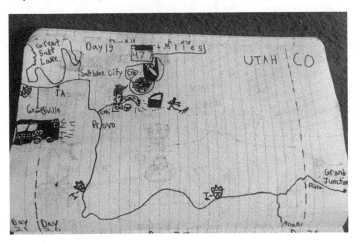

7/15/15 Day 23 Wednesday

Crashed out for a few hours of sleep in the front seat. Then bounced out for a sec and the guys were in front so I half slept in the parking lot and when that was no longer working went to get a hot chocolate and check gas prices. Main man train-hoppin was curled with his dog next to the Dodge Ram. Kyle awoke first and lay down in the parking lot in a much better mood than the day before. Gas chugged and aired up a tire and we were off. Getting the fuck out of Utah finally. Kyle started to seethe in the driver's seat. His whole body tightened. His knuckles went white gripping the steering wheel. The long hours driving, lack of a woman, and being pissed at how the past relationship went down fueled his frustration. He hopped out, as usual. No shoes on with Johnny and me hopping out after, bringing the ole bean bag from the van encouraging him to punch the shit out of it till he got some rage out.

Casinos at every gas station in Nevada. Repeated the gas-chugging, spanging and gambling at each one along the way. I hopped out with the two young guys hitting the Walmart for provisions. I picked up some peanut butter, cans of beans for energy, basic rations like any other day and looked up with a mischievous eye to see the guys rolling around on the handicap scooters. They bumped into each other and raced around the store. Johnny said, "This woman with her boyfriend was checking me out and he's getting pissed." Seeing the punk boys atop the scooters an older man yells out to them, "You're a disgrace!" He's probably just a man running errands in his structured life and they're two poor young guys just trying to get some fun and enjoyment out of life.

Different ways to look at life the perspective of the punk boys in Walmart to the older man doing his shopping thinking them obnoxious. Who's right? What kind of life is this at a Walmart? With all these cheap products, cheap wages. How sci-fi is this big box poorly-lit place?

Got stopped by the cops doing 82 in a 65. Kyle didn't have a license. Said they were headed back home to Sac and Cali in general. And the cops let us off and said that I could drive as I had a legit one and at least Kyle had the registration. The OG license holder had to kick rocks for the moment.

At a tobacco rez shop, Isiah fit in for a change. Shitty cigar in hand everyone else had cigs smoking away as the car flies down I-80. Kyle back driving and cigar ash spraying here n there messily. A motorcyclist is spotted. Kyle signaled to her two fingers to mouth seeing if she had weed, she signaled back the same signal. Both vehicles pull over in the breakdown lane. She thought we had weed we thought she had. Said she knows where to get some. The Ram follows then stops at another gas station. I grabbed beers for the crew. She comes in the van gets introduced cracks one and plans to stow the bike and head to the rainbow gathering in Washington with the guys. Stopped outside a prison for a break. She made sure to hide her red hair in her helmet as we were in the county where there were two warrants out for her arrest one of them a domestic for beating up her girlfriend the other no recollection comes to mind. Then we headed to her friend's place. Kyle's spirits are lifted with the aberrance of another badass chick. I flipped a penny and say, "Heads she's gay." Don't find the penny. Passed by Reno on the way in train-hopper keeps opening yelling out the window and he can project like a former carny, "Step right up and try to get the ring around the bottle!" A biker going by with skull mouth bandanna and pith helmet we look like something out of *Road Warrior* crossing the desert. In the flow, bliss.

Rocket from The Tombs playing in the back of my head,
"Ain't it fun when you're always on the run
Ain't it fun when your friends despise what you've become
Ain't it fun when you get so high
Well…that you just can't come
Ain't it fun when you know that you're gonna die young
It's such fun."

We get to her friend's place and smoke up. She hops in the car and we're off. She learns quick and quickly becomes one of the best gas chuggers especially with the older white guys who become the most giving. They see an attractive young woman who seems in need to them and they cannot resist loosening their wallets to help. Kyle drives and drives. He pulls over to stop for the night, but I push him onward seeing my buddy Jon's house is only sixty exits away. Struggle to stay awake. Arriving with two in the van now immobile given the time. Jon greets us warmly and sells hash oil to the guys which they dab on the end of their cigarettes and smoke upwardly. Jon and Liz his girlfriend hang out and offer drinks and Jon shows with a model what the structure of methamphetamine and ecstasy is, wowing the guys. Jon presents it as only a chemist who works with drugs on a daily basis can.

Bid farewell as they drive off to a parking lot to crash leaving my boots rain gear and one or two other items in the car.

What's the price this traveling life takes? The toll includes alcoholism, drugs>heroin. The music ahh the music. How different is a traveler clique from other cliques? The pit bull, the dirty kid rag, the sign a flying, the spanging, the outsider mentality, the escapism, the adventure, the hardship, and the wheels on the track or road spin to oblivion. How different is it from any other group of people attempting to temporarily function together? The details are different, but I still don't know if there is much difference in the big picture.

7/16-17/15 Day 24-25 Thursday-Friday

Next Evening. Jon, Liz and I headed to Sac to get steins and sausages. Sac is shorthand for Sacramento. Woman with a noticeably annoying SoCal accent went on about my dreads and proceeded to make out sloppily with the man across from her at the end of her drink. "That an $1.50 buys ya a cup a coffee." Yes and… Finally hit a dive in Sac for a last drink and left.

Next night after relating stories of travel and zoning out in front of Jon's homemade screen we headed west to the suburbs of Oakland. After a short random bar experience of bikers, the young the old and what have you with other displaced characters, we met two of his guy friends, went to a rocking dive with a live band and a loose Louisiana mother who said she'd redo my dreads like her husband. I set off a mortar in the parking lot and drove out to a park and we set off the rest of the mortars. Jon's friends set off things that looked like sparklers but when thrown, shoot off in a random direction. Went and crashed at my cousin's in Oakland who had been out dancing all night.

7/18/15 Day 26 Saturday

The next day still regrettably I took the train instead of hitchhiking down to Menlo Park. I got an image in my head I would hitch all the way to Santa Cruz and have an epic dive of victory into the water. The town is a Richie Rich land of sorts with the highest median income in the country. I call Tim my friend from second grade and get picked up by him and his girlfriend at the market.

"You know there's money when there are white people performing free music from Zimbabwe and an unmarked Facebook tent is giving away a free coffee table book of its in-house artists." Quite a drastic change from what and who I had been interacting with for the most part on the journey as delusions of grandeur appeared before mine eyes. As always adaptions had to be made, not always smoothly, to interact in this new environment. So far from day-to-day survival with the exception of those who come in to work daily here. The everyday workers were not of this place and took long journeys to different worlds not colored in such Nuevo modernist, veiled progressive, technocratic finery.

Does life need to be sustainable or just get you there? The place you want or need to go. How useful are survival skills out here if everything just went to hell? Are they applicable in a blackout? In a disaster? When there's no direction home.

Headed back to his place then drove down to Santa Cruz to finish off the trip. Tried to tamp down being pissed off at the overuse of technology by my friend and his girlfriend in trying to pay the meter, instead of going to change quarters and being done with it. Finally, on the beach, Tim said something I found inhibiting in my present mood. Said classically "That's how the terrorists win" and run n dove in the ocean. We had always been very different people, but I had the rising concern and somewhat revulsion at the moment, that the corporate new age technocrats of Silicon had sucked him into their ways of individual isolation. He even disapproved of rolling down the windows on the way in when it threatened his comfort and controlled environment. Tim in his past was no stranger to extreme outdoor climates. Comin back at him was probably what he perceived to be a wild man with a known penchant for hating control.

How is it to see your childhood friends become something at odds with who you now are? Tim with the windows cloistered in technology comfort land. My friend since kindergarten Dan back in New York working for a company that helps Coca Cola advertise. They become part of a corporate world and life you had no liking for and were repulsed by instinctually from the youngest of ages. A person navigates the world in absolute compliance with its dictates, or in opposition and subversion, using what is necessary to avoid its persistent hunger for pure consumption and allegiance to the brand, the company.

Refreshed I came out of the ocean Tim dug a hole in the sand and I got stuck in it with just my head sticking out. Good to see him nostalgic, and good for me, too. Then we had a meal at a local restaurant the recent feelings fading away into the food for the time.

7/19/15 Day 27 Sunday

Had breakfast with the couple and drank the beer of triumph. My friend Michael the trucker had given me that tenner to buy it with. I called him and told him I had reached my destination, Santa Cruz. He was pleased to hear it. Tim dropped me off at Millbrae BART. Came into the Mission walked up to a bar friendly to dogs and wrote part of this there and the last bit of the journal at the Rogue brewhouse near Chinatown.

   Momentum had carried me onward right into the Pacific. The momentum carried me to write the last line of notes written at the bars. Momentum from point A to point P, from the Atlantic to the Pacific. Endurance and momentum had gotten me this far. They had gotten me to reach my long-sought goal of hitching all of the way cross country. But now I had met that goal. And the time had come. The time to, the time to?

Part II

Part II

Chapter 10

Out of Chinatown, I go. Up and down and finally down further still I go to the docks. To Frisco's well-water-worn exit point. The trip that I had thought about for the past few years ended. I looked out over the bay as it churned, the future uncertain. The time arrived to fanshen, to turn into the wind, to turn over, to free myself, to bring a change to my fortunes and see the world's various complexions.

The time to head back across the bay to see my cousin Sone came to pass. Sone has lived in Oakland for years now. Ever since she started at her all women's college, Mills, where she'd earned her Master's Degree, she had become more outspoken. So outspoken that when she was chosen to give the main speech at her college graduation, she savvily brought attention to fellow graduation speaker Nancy Pelosi's lack of the use of the word transgender. I watched as my cousin Sone made her challenge, with her mortarboard on and her long brown curls hanging over her right shoulder, "To widen the potential paths through Mills to reflect our experiences and potentials as queer and transgender students."

The start of her speech was dripping with sarcasm about the present. "May 2010 sounded pretty futuristic until today. 2010 sounded like a year in the movie you know. Cars you can plug in, a mixed-race black president, a nearly dystopic state of world affairs, a world without Michael Jackson and yet here we are throttled into the future our future. Graduating from college amidst these fantastical plot lines. Thankfully here at Mills we like to think of this Orwellian story as a choose your own ending type of adventure." I guess Nancy had felt derided by my dear cousin and decided to add to her own speech. Later in the graduation, she didn't actually say this, but from what I recall about the Speaker of the House's address she'd said something to the tune of, "Sonya you know the future is not that dark… After all, I am the first woman to be Speaker of the House." I guess my cuz's speech had an effect on Nancy.

I called Sone, "Hey cuz I'm headed across the Bay to come see ya."

She said, "Oh ok, me and Rosie are at a festival outside the Bay, but we'll be back in a few hours." Sonya and Rosie had been together as girlfriends for a few years now. My sister-in-law had mentioned to me recently that they were one of the few couples she trusted to take care of her kids. I remembered how they both showed so much care and affection for my niece when Sone and my brother attended my graduation from Prescott College. My family took a break before my graduation and walked along a desert path outside of Prescott. The tall dusty rocks edged the side of the lake, while the spring grass wrapped around the rest of the lake. My brother and my niece walked together. Then, as my six-year-old niece got more comfortable, she went with Sonya and Rosie as they picked up rocks and looked around the banks. Sonya and Rosie both kept a close eye on my little niece Mia, they played and looked out for her with care and tended to her so she would stay on shore. The water I looked at now went deeper and stretched farther than that lake, but it lacked the reflection of the Arizona sun and was hidden below a mist. I viewed it from a distance.

Took the ferry across to Oakland, feeling free with the breeze ruffling my shirt, the bay churning beneath, and the lights only barely visible in the distance. I planned to see a few friends and family along the way. I would head north to see Sheba along the coast in Fort Bragg. Sheba became a friend after we both didn't make the cut for an internship in Florida. She is small with dark-rimmed glasses and has a love for shelled sea creatures. She is blunt and honest about how she feels and this has led to both positive and negative responses throughout her life. We last parted ways at a train station in south Florida. Onward from Fort Bragg and Sheba, I planned to visit Julia in Portland. Julia and I met as fellow interns and co-instructors for Outward Bound Baltimore and Philadelphia. She is tall for a woman with short quirky hair and a quirky attitude to match. She has a wide smile and girlish laugh along with a love for wanderous ways, ways akin to mine. And O how her smile and laugh can bring warmth and light into a room. A visit to her would most likely be the most northern point of the second part of this journey while the most southern point remained elusive.

While I wanted to hitch, I yielded to other modes of travel as well. The absolutist way of purely thumbing rides I had committed to only for the first part of my journey. I moved along just fine in this way and traveled by other cheap means, from getting rides to using public transportation. I had previous experiences taking Greyhound rides cross country. I traversed Colorado and the central time zone in a big white shuttle van when I was in AmeriCorps. (From Wikipedia's definition, "AmeriCorps is a voluntary civil society program supported by the U.S. federal government, foundations, corporations, and other donors engaging adults in public service work with a goal of helping others and meeting critical needs in the community.") This past exposure helped to a degree but did not give me a precise roadmap.

How I would travel down from Oregon still remained cloudy. Would I hit the bay again or go directly to see Ra in LA? I met Ra on the first day of orientation at Prescott College. Since I had known him he had become a peer and a mentor to me on subjects near and far. LA also brought a potential job connection from a heroin-riddled Scotsman who was one hell of a painter. I had briefly worked with this man in Boston, and he told me about a relative who had a successful construction business in Los Angeles.

One thing I did know before I'd even left for the trip, I wanted to get a zoot suit. I looked up a store in Fullerton, CA and wrote down the address and phone number. It seemed like I'd done that ages ago, but in reality, it had been less than a month.

I would be traveling more east at this point as I exited Fullerton. My only thought was that my next two points of contact would be Ben in Flagstaff and Matteo in New Mexico. Ben a more reliable possibility while Matteo definitely held the key to fun, but harder to pin down being a creative and more unpredictable spirit. So arrived the general outline of the plan as I took in the salty air and watched the yellow night lights from Oakland elucidate the small traces of water that hugged the bay's coast.

The water that ringed the ferry rippled in the black darkness. The engine and the foghorn prevailed as the only forces intruding on the bay this night. This next trip begins as the other ends. The first a momentum-bound haul with a set goal in mind. The second a deeper relational voyage into the unknown.

I stopped in at a bar near my cousin's place. The bartender got annoyed at one of her wannabe macho customers spreading his personal effluvia around for all to hear in the bar. She confided her displeasure,

"I just wish some people could handle their drink."

I fake machoed myself a little by raising my shoulders puffing out my chest and said, "Let me know if you want anything done."

She said, "No."

I gave him the evil eye and he approached me with a lean and small stumble. He started to slur his words in my direction. At least the attention was off her. Eventually, he left. And, as the night moved like molasses with few customers to speak of, we got to talking. I offered my hand across the bar and in turn, she offered hers. Our hands clasped firmly yet softly over the wood of the bar. She had dreadlocks like me, body on the shorter side, a little thick, and sparkling light blue eyes.

"I'm Shay," she said.

"Alex."

"What are you doing around here?"

"Well, I'm hitchin' on thru right now, though I'm stayin' with my cousin right nearby." It definitely seemed to help her openness to me to tell her I was staying at my cousin's close by.

"I'm going hiking tomorrow," she said.

"Could I tag along?"

Shay calmly said, "Yeah."

It turned out she played music professionally from time to time and tomorrow would be her birthday. With a light buzz, I headed to Rosie and Sone's in search of restful sleep, hopeful for tomorrow.

Morning materialized and excitement grew in my beer-addled stomach. I awoke in Sone and Rosie's cushy couch in their living room. A low hardwood table to my right, a long hallway into the kitchen behind my head and warm colors and plants blurring into my vision seemingly everywhere. The time for the date's arrival beckoned soon. Before I left, Rosie looked out for my interests and told me to "Take a few beers from their fridge." And then she opened up a little pouch of weed and handed it to me.

"Thanks," I said, and smiled back at her.

Shay picked me up and we drove off back into the hills. On the way, we picked up a skateboarder who slalomed down the hill and thumbed his way back up. We reached the top of the hill and started to descend. There down from the road a tiny historic train in the woods chugged its way onward. We hopped on the train and took the small tour as a novelty. I just felt good to be outside and I thought Shay did too as I saw a smile creep from the sides of her mouth, the light flickering through green leaves on the hot day. Both of our legs got crammed in the little train car fit for kids and my big knees poked out. I thought not a bad way to build rapport as our legs brushed together.

After the train ride, we drove down to a trailhead. We hiked around a bit ascending and descending the hot forested trails. We passed by a small lake and ventured uphill further into the woods. We came back down to the small lake from the other side. The water cooled my feet although heated ire drifted close by. The lifeguards would yell across at ya if they saw you taking a dip outside the designated zone. There along the bank lay a grouping of rocks, and people with plentiful dogs at play. Being out west, I could see once again a preponderance of pit mixes. Shay stood ankle deep in the lake, while I lowered myself all the way in to cool off.

After we hiked around the edge of the lake, we came upon a tree with a platform splayed between its branches. We climbed the tree. Then we sat alongside each other with our backs propped up by the large trunk.

Shay said, "I'd really like a beer,"

I popped a couple out of my bag.

Her face lit up slightly surprised, then pleased, then she smiled over at me. We sipped on the beers looking out over the lake in the tree-filtered light, relaxing. We both got up and took separate tree limbs to lie down on. We laid across from each other before climbing out further still. Only air and a fifteen-foot drop was between us. We laid down even further out and I imagined a painting from a bird's-eye view of our bodies outstretched balancing on the sun-caressed tree.

After a few minutes, I said, "I'm coming over."

Our eyes met. She looked confused. I came over and, truth be told, it was awkward. I did some sort of modified push-up over her on the branch and kissed her. She kissed me back. The second time I kissed her it still felt awkward. We moved back to the platform. We sat, drank beers and made out, the kissing improved.

She had to go to work so we headed back.

I told her I'd meet her later that evening at the bar.

I picked up a piece of cake at the supermarket across from the bar. Then I went into the bar with the plastic bag with cake tucked behind my back. She bartended and her other friends and customers mingled at the bar. She introduced me and they all seemed real friendly. They took the candle that had been on a cookie for Shay and put it on my piece of cake. The chocolate cake fit the celebration better than the sweet cookie. In the course of the night, many drinks guzzled greedily as they disappeared down the throats of their patrons. At closing time I helped stack chairs onto tables as Shay cleaned up the bar. Right as she finished the cleanup, she pulled out her guitar. She strategically had made sure that two chairs at the end of the bar remained right side up. She sat down and started to play and sing one of her own songs that I don't remember the name of, but the lyrics cast the mood dark and troubled. I liked it. I felt flattered by her willingness to share so openly with me.

In the present moment at this point in my journey as my head drifted outside my body to the music the only word that comes to mind is surreal. For the time had come, the middle of the trip when going back seemed just as long as going forward. Time stretched in even lengths behind and ahead. The future and the past equidistant with equally burdensome weight. This thought arrived heavy and bent my mind. The visceral strength of the moment gave me a feeling of weightlessness at the same time. The moment ingrained its mark deep inside; etching the low-lit room, the upside-down barstools, the wood-lined floor, and her vital eyes, into me.

We headed over to her friend's place round about three in the morning. Her friend was a laugh. A tall Iranian or South Asian woman who constantly got herself into dating drama. Her words flowed freely and she wore a bright red dress and heels. She looked like a girly girl, but her wit and her sailor mouth colored the apartment.

"Bitch, whore, cunt, Where's the weed?"

I smoked along with everyone else. Shay did coke. I've never done nor had the attraction to the white stuff. For I am a downer man and honestly in spite of the way I look not the most chemically exploratory.

We finally made it back to Shay's near cracking dawn, smoked her bong, and passed the fuck out. Our heads hit the pillow like bricks thrown into the bay. I didn't sleep much. Blearily I remembered Shay had told me to wake her up because of a camping trip she had planned for tomorrow. I rustled and droningly told her, "Shay... Shaaaay... you... need... to... get... u-u-up."

We had sex. I initiated it feeling her up moving through to doggy style. Although it was her birthday that arrived this morning she still finished me off nicely. Surprisingly kind of her I thought. If anyone decided to go down on anyone I thought it would be me and my tongue on her special day. I felt an animalistic purity about the sex. I had been on the road with nothing in the way of close physical affection and finally, Shay had granted me a release. Waiting that long for sex and without being distracted by screens or sexual illusions I realized that I had been purely in the moment. It felt so good, now there was a different question: what to do with all that focused energy?

She snoozed back for a little bit and I noticed a poster of a half-naked women across from the bed which started to raise questions in my mind.

We went over to her friend's apartment, who was somehow running even later than us. We picked up her and her dog and headed out to Modesto. We met up with her promoter friend there and then went to a future concert venue. We arrived at an area of tree-lined land owned by this guy who paved roads for money. But when we arrived we didn't even see him. He had collected all sorts of sculptures and a sizeable plot of mixed desert to forested land along the Tuolumne River. A concert date later in the month had already been set. Shay would perform. After we set up a tent a short walk from the main house I found myself on this hot sunny day floating in the river and swinging out on the rope swing surrounded by women once again in my life. I had grown up with my mothers and their female friends' always coming by the house for visits. They both had sisters and the only other guys in the family I saw growing up were my older brother Dan and my grandfathers on the occasional trips we made to my grandparents. The old familiar feeling of comfort and partial suffocation set in being around all these women. I knew how to relate, but at times I needed to put in some extra effort to make this happen. I felt that territory of my own needed to be staked out for the just cause of mental sanity. In the end, the old familiar cyclical nature of this situation would replay itself. That is how it seemed to me, only a bit less fatalistic.

A young woman and her loud cheerful fellow resident arrived at the river. This loud woman reminded me of my neighbor growing up. Affable with freewheeling outspoken attitude and a smoker and drinker. The young woman friendly, but definitely out there with her dog barking away and the two of them together a smatter of barking and abrupt run-on sentences. She seemed to talk in tangents. In one of her tangents, I found out that she was the wife of the man out paving. The man who had not been sharing in this experience with all these women. The man not here because he was out working hard keeping the place running with the money he made. Still, his absence felt strong. The young woman probably twenty years younger than him inhabited this strange place. When she invited us into her house, she made sure to show each one of us a book of pictures of different vaginas. The home constructed of wood made me feel warm and comfortable. Even better yet she put in an order for pizza. We hung out and the promoter played videos on her iPhone of singers and bands that she and her son liked.

After the pizza and drinking, Shay's friend wondered where she had gone and I went to look. I checked the tent we had set. No Shay. I looked around still no Shay. I couldn't find her. I got a little concerned and wondered where she had gone and why she hadn't told me? Her promoter friend mentioned she went off sometimes by herself. Checking in the tent again I decided to just go to sleep. The temperature still burned the skin, but luckily we had put the tent in an area hemmed in by tall leafy trees. The branches hung over and reduced the temperature by about twenty degrees. I felt some relief at rest and stopped wrestling with my own thoughts though Shay's absence still bothered me.

Come morning, I awoke and found that Shay had been sleeping out in one of the hammocks near the river. She seemed to be pulling away with her distance and lack of communication. We hadn't seen each other and then when we did talk only a few words were exchanged. It had been over twelve hours. The last time I thought we both got along had been at the rope swing. We packed up to go and said our goodbyes. I said goodbye to the young woman who talked in tangents and her dog. She hugged me longer than usual. I thought that although she never said it, she wanted a man closer to her age that would let her flourish in her own right. At that moment, I could have kissed her. She also had a way about her that spoke of someone who may have been involved in a cult at one time. Or maybe still. My impression of her could have also been due to the setting. Country California brings to my mind ole Charlie Manson and communes gone wrong. When I left the concert venue my hunger began to grow. The heat, dehydration, and anger all mixed together and I started to get hangry. The trip on the dusty road out towards civilization only exacerbated this feeling.

We stopped for burritos and I started to ego trip over being famished. I didn't show care for Shay. All I could think of was my own nourishment. I pretty much ignored whatever conversation the women were having. Being around different people once again for an extended length of time had grown tiresome. My eyes grew as I saw my burrito alone and the orange Jarritos coming out of the fridge. The part of my mind that wasn't focused on food allowed me to simply get through this social interaction. Shay looked away more often than before. Even the conversation in the car flowed more easily with her friend with the dog. We at least had the east coast in common. Shay dropped me off outside of Sone's, we kissed, agreeing to see each other soon. She drove off to her place and I headed up the driveway.

When I got back to Sone's apartment the relationship between her and Rosie felt clearly off. I felt like air had ceased to flow through the rooms. They gave furtive looks that only seemed to tighten each one of them. Rosie sat in a chair, with her back bent and would give overly polite replies as if everything was fine. Sone moved around. She never stayed in one place too long. When she spoke her mouth crooked and she spoke in short bursts. I felt the tension all around.

When I visited a few years before, Rosie had been much quieter. Sone's role was as the constant principled verbalizer who smoothly made her point. As always she had demonstrated her skill at communication. It made no difference if the topic was politics, women's or queer rights, or just talking about her friends in the Bay. She had of course been in motion, but her movements seemed to be purposeful and most of the time didn't seem laden with too much anxiety. This time she moved just as much as before, but it was as if her motions and decisions were caught in static. This extended to her speech which colored the room with its underlying aggravation. Rosie carried on calmly though she was clearly affected by Sone's mood. This lasted until Sonya left the house in a quietly resigned huff. In the course of the day I tried to ignore the unignorable mood and catch up a bit with each one of them on their own. Mostly though I just rested, planning for the next northern haul.

I saw Shay once more at the bar before I left. I did intend to see her again upon my return to the Bay area from the Pacific Northwest, but who knows how I would feel then? The script had yet to been written. For the moment though it would be good to see her and more than this it felt good to have a connection to someone that wasn't just a friend or family in the Bay. The brightness of the midday outside contrasted sharply with the darkness of the bar she inhabited inside. She tended the bar and I just looked like any other midday boozer customer. She poured me Guinness and I sat and drank it.

I said, "I'll be back in a couple weeks after I go see friends up north."

We looked into each other's eyes. Displeasure, but also care seemed to play across her face. She poured me another Guinness and we kissed. I headed to the nearest station and on to Richmond on BART. Back to the same old again. Back to sleeping down from the on-ramp.

The morning arrived and in quick succession, I got picked up by a couple of nondescript drivers. First a Chicano guy in a t-shirt. Next a younger retiree picked me up and I headed further north. Then waiting in Santa Rosa a Chicano family picked me up. I lucked out their direction matched up perfectly. We both wanted to head directly to Fort Bragg. The family consisted of a mother and her two teenage daughters. I talked mainly with the older daughter since the mother only spoke Spanish but we tried to exchange pleasantries. I communicated in my mangled Spanglish. The older daughter inhabited both worlds the best because she was fluently bilingual. She translated from time to time. Internally I found entertainment easily. All I had to do live and wonder. We stopped at a gas station and I really wondered what people thought. What the hell is this scruffy guy doing with this family? We drove west from Willits through the Jackson State Forest. We went up over the hills and descended down to Fort Bragg. The road changed from the hot 101 to the cooler woods which transformed and descended back to the ocean. I wished them well as they dropped me off in the center of Fort Bragg and I started walking down the street toward the cliffs.

I walked down a side street as I explored the town. The first guy I met hanging out on an empty street corner. He called over to me, a hippie drunk dad to be. He immediately started going on affably about the supernatural and his realization that soon he would be a father. In return, I told him a short bit about myself. Amazed by me on account of my hitching story we hugged finally and he took his leave going back toward town as I headed to the beach. The beach held treasures different from most other beaches thanks to a now defunct bottling plant that sat up from the beach.

I found the glass beach covered in multicolored broken gems as if a storm causing shipwreck had splayed a pirate's bounty to rest upon the shore. The smoothed glass felt good and cool on my feet. As I looked up from my feet families appeared all around me. My obliviousness had taken hold. I'd had tunnel vision on my arrival at the beach, so focused on cooling my road-weary feet. I ate my peanut butter and beans. Aside from the families, other creatures started to make their presence known. The damn squirrels of the cliffs started to poke their heads out and came with sniveling nostrils out to try to grab a bite. They must have lived in the holey sides of the base of the rocky cliffs. I repeatedly threw my shoes at them. I picked my shoes back up and pretended with shoes raised that a good clobbering was just around the corner. I burned a good amount of energy, expending most of what I had gotten from my meal. They kept harassing me throughout the meal and finally fucked off a little when I finished.

It seemed like a while since the last time I had seen Sheba. There'd been a moment back in Florida on that beach in Lake Worth. Our eyes met, hers shining green in the glittering light as we treaded water facing each other in the warm Atlantic. Nothing had come of it.

I knew Sheba had yet to arrive in town. She planned to come back to her residence the next day. I learned to my pleasant surprise that the North Coast brewery had materialized in town and I headed to their restaurant. The order came in and was voluminous when it showed up. A thirteen glass sampler of most of the beers they had on hand. I struck up a conversation with the older woman sitting across from me. I saw her eyeing my bounty. The conversation drifted off and she left. By this time my buzz from the sampler had grown and so did my openness to fellow patrons still seated nearby. I met a muscle-bound, handsome, but strange guy.

We hit another bar and he told me, "I do not have a good history with women."

I talked to a fun couple and came around to the guy's side.

The boyfriend asked lightheartedly, "Is your friend hitting on my girlfriend?"

I said, "Well I just met the guy. I don't think so."

He visibly relaxed and it looked good for the nice strange guy to just be having a normal conversation with a woman.

The strange guy and I exchanged numbers, having found ourselves to be both tourists alone in a new town. I pushed through the crowded bar unceremoniously. My ungainly sleeping bag, mat, and backpack bumped into people. They threw back complaints.

"Hey man, what are you doing!"

"What the fuck is this!"

Stumbling out toward the cliffs I suddenly had to go, had to, right now! My bowels rumbled and pressure built. I stepped over the little barrier onto the protected grassy wildflower cliffs and shit my bowels out explosively as I tried to avoid the fall down the side of the cliff. Feeling relieved but disgusted, I fell asleep curled up in my sleeping bag and mat underneath a park bench and on top of the cliffs. The wind strong, the stars bright, the ocean loud and I became unconscious. With darkness, the shining glass below remained destitute to my vision.

The next day I cleaned up myself slowly. I moved into the goosebumps-inducing water as a young man taught a young woman how to snorkel. They had smartly donned full-length thick wetsuits.

I met Sheba at her place less than a half mile from where I had slept the night before. She lowered her voice so others could not hear and made sure to fill me in on a key detail before I entered her place.

"You can stay at my place," she said. "I'm gonna stay at my boyfriend's, we're keeping it quiet though."

She lived in a small one-room apartment perfect for her stature, but a tight fit for me. Sheba and her undercover boyfriend were hiding their relationship from the landlady because she held some old-fashioned ideas. For example, the landlord would invite Sheba's boyfriend over for a gentlemen's dinner where he would have to act all proper. He was weirded out by the proposition of giving an archaic dinner party performance to his landlord. Additionally the expectation of a Victorian gender role Sheba could not quite unqueer to. When the landlord came by she would hop back to her room. The boyfriend seemed nice enough and a good fit with Sheba's geekiness.

We originally met on a training course for Outward Bound at-risk youth outside of Orlando. We both failed to receive contracts for the internship and me thinks it had to do with having a personality and not being in lockstep with what the trainers wanted. They gave us the option to stay the night to figure it out. We hightailed it the fuck out of there in Sheba's small bright green car. We didn't stop until we saw a museum of marine invertebrates. We both felt upset about the cut from the internship. Sheba more so than I. The museum provided a respite from what we had just been through. Sheba loved geeking out over complex creatures of the natural world. It helped both of us as we needed to destress and focus on something completely different.

After the museum, we stopped and got some fast food at a local joint. We felt a bit better about ourselves after eating and having a bitch session. The time came to part ways. She dropped me off at the nearest train station as I headed to seek the unknown Miami. She went her way towards her father's house in South Florida. Thereafter I came back up north a couple times from Miami. There occurred even one time where I saw her sparkling eyes as we treaded water across from each other on another hot Florida day and in that moment I could have kissed her. The moment passed and she still had a distant boyfriend at the time. It had been some time and she now found herself working a much steadier job on the other coast after being through the wringer of outdoor work.

Sheba and I went over to her friend's organic farm to volunteer and to see if I could work out some kind of exchange to stay for a little while. When I met her friend she gave me a warm flirtatious hug which struck an interest. I asked Sheba later about her friend and she said that she had a longtime girlfriend, but also saw a guy from time to time who Sheba hated for being sexist. Her friend's flirtation came as no surprise to Sheba.

"She does that with everybody."

At the farm worked a young Australian guy who labored alongside his girlfriend, he had taken his summer break and come out from college in New York.

Sheba dropped me off at the farm. On that day, the tomatoes made our hands black with their residue. The young woman, the Australian, and I prepared them for the farmer's market. The Australian and I drove on in and started to fumble with the tent. The wind blew, the tent opened incompletely. Finally, the young woman came over. She scolded us for our ignorance and showed us how to make the tent easily erect.

The tent standing, the food organized, Sheba stopped by, customers stopped by. I said farewell got one more warm hug from the young woman and headed to Sheba's place. That hug still runs through my mind. Her body pressed closely up against mine. My arms wrapped around her shoulders. Hands wrapped around my lower back. This consummate farewell lingered with its warm sensuousness. We would not meet again.

Sheba and I went out to eat and watched the movie *Train Wreck* laughing away at the funny ridiculous performances. After the laughter, Sheba became quiet and looked around. Her brow wrinkled with frustration.

"There's racists in this town," she said. She said she missed being around other black and brown people. She had an African mother and a mixed Asian father. Fort Bragg definitely seemed a hell of a lot different than her former residence in more diverse, southern Florida. We talked of our separate times in AmeriCorps and how, in her experience, "Most black corps leaders left or are forced out before their contract was up."

"It's nutty," I said.

I knew the job as a corps leader already held tough enough responsibilities. I had seen how it affected my own stressed corps leader and all the drama that can happen when 18- to 24-year-olds travel and live together in close confines. I had been a more effortful member of the rank and file to deal with. The role of corps leader or team leader for a group required an ability to look after a number of young adults whose age only differed moderately from Sheba's. The job worsened because she lacked support from her higher-ups.

We watched music videos at her place mostly hip hop and R&B, especially Janelle Monae the multitalented singer, dancer, and all-around performer. Sheba loved her rhythm, style, playfulness, and voice. And she thought that Janelle had made one of the gayest sorority house videos ever. Hmm... I thought to myself. Something Sheba had said about her and the girl who was seeing the Australian struck me,

"We're all just hiding our queerness."

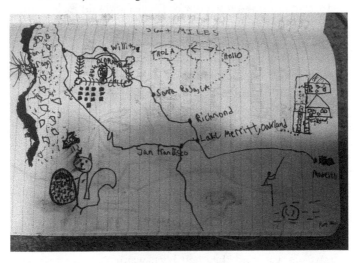

I said farewell in the morning as Sheba left for work and I gathered my things from her place. I walked out to State Route 1 which goes thru Fort Bragg and got picked up within a mile by an old man smoking weed and tobacco. He drove me out to the beach in his convertible. I looked out over the cliffs one last time.

Cheerful enough character, he adapted his route and dropped me off northward. Shortly thereafter I hopped in with a couple of hippie Buddhist young guys. We stopped by a tourist attraction a big ole redwood and joke talked about life then continued on our way. They explained their Buddhist beliefs and talked about their communal living situation. Both guys kind Nor Cal spoken, one Asian one white. Both more at peace than their grit full increasingly patience strained passenger. This listener could not or didn't wanted to shake his reactive Northeast action-oriented temperament.

The Buddhists left me at another forgettable supermarket to resupply and chow down for lunch. I had lost my can opener and brutally smashed open my beans with a sharp rock. Definitely back to the bare living.

I walked through town out of Eureka and said fuck it when rides refused to appear and started walking on the highway to Arcata. As I continued to walk the road, Arcata became clear well into the distance. There were piney trees to the right and seawater with a curved coastline to Arcata on the left. I passed by a small airport and eventually obtained a ride from a young surf kid coming back from Hawaii and a black dudebro who didn't take off his sunglasses the entire ride. He recommended I stay in Arcata for a while. "You might not leave," he said.

Well, I saw the center of town with travelers, summer college students, some money, hippies, and back up the street a nice old-fashioned movie theater. I made the decision that I should stay elsewhere. Arcata had a definite beauty and comfort to it. I also got the sense I would be lulled into a state of amnesia and misdirected off my path for who knows how long. I talked to travelers who said they had been waiting almost two days for a ride. But they appeared a little scragglier than I was and had massive backpacks. I passed them by and walked onward. I tried my luck at the next on-ramp up and got a ride just a few towns northward from a friendly college student.

Then I got a ride through town from a guy who told me where to go in a couple months for the trimming season, known also as the best time to make money harvesting marijuana.

The next ride fit well from a bearded mountain man who worked out in the forests and had somewhat of a troublesome leg. He told me that this area had great hunting and fishing.

He said, "You know with the amount of salmon Indians catch up on the rez around here, they can buy a new truck each year." My interest was piqued when he told me about the bounty of fish. I wondered how accurate his information could really be. He reassured me the amount of fish to money stood true as we rolled on down the rural route. He dropped me on a dirt road with nothing immediately around it except an open field and trees.

I took a look back and a few shops materialized, spaced out back behind me. Farmland on my right side with forest on the left. Its coniferous borders surrounded this little bit of civilization. The sun started to go down and I could see woods in the distance, I started to think about camp. Another gamble emerged on the horizon. Should I stay and camp or try to go further onward as the light dimmed through the trees? Lo and behold, a truck with its shell on top pulled on up with a hardy older but slightly suspicious lady peering out. When I went for the door she said I could get in the back. It ended up being me and the dog hangin' out peaceably enough back there. She dropped me at the gas station near a casino and the wheels started to turn. See if I couldn't turn a few bucks and crash out.

My casino and plans for sleep remained unfulfilled. As a young woman asked if I needed a ride and could I throw down a few bucks. I agreed after hearing their destination was to drive well into Oregon. The young woman and two younger guys made up her crew. One of them twenty and able-bodied, the other seventeen and who fit the definition of seventeen being slim and lazy yet still exhibiting an entitled attitude. The last member of the car was another mutt of a traveling dog. They had just come from glass beach as I had. She had three kids to get back to in Oregon. She and the guys had gotten a chance to go out and about and have a change of scenery from home. They had collected some glass pieces on their little adventure. She used to ride the rails and knew all about it. She'd had enough of that life and possibly the man or men who had led to the kids. The twenty-year-old made a positive impression on me, he seemed to be a giving, smart, strong, resourceful guy who had a rough life through foster care.

When we stopped at a gas station in Oregon, I chatted up the drive-thru store attendants hoping for money, aid, or information, but it led to nothing. The twenty-year-old wasn't having much luck either. He held a sign while his dog looked a bit bedraggled. The young woman tried to hit up customers at the gas station, the only problem being that in Oregon (and in Jersey too, not that it mattered), you can't pump your own gas. The attendants are on you if you try to get some money or gas out of other customers. She tried to sneakily ask customers as they pulled around. The real money came when I won some money at the slot machine and the twenty-year-old found another $20 outside of the store, close to the store's garbage can ashtray.

We detoured a ways off the main road to some hot springs at the base of mountains. The fire could be seen as it smoldered in patches which illuminated the forest from the road. The smell of smoke filled my nostrils. We had to be led as if by a pace car down the road past the danger zone by the flashing light of the forestry truck. To the left side of the road, small patches of orange visibly floated in the distance smoldering away. The flames stayed static and contained. It smelled like a giant campfire. In the car everyone's hands tensed, our eyes became acutely aware. Eventually, though, the lights ahead of us moved to the left. The pace car stopped and we sailed past the land of smoke. Finally, the time had come to relax. The long day had extended past midnight.

We arrived at the bottom of the trail to the hot springs. We got out of the car and hiked up the hill. We rounded the bend and clutched the railing which guided us down the path and there they lay; the springs formed small pools of different temperatures. The cooler one seemed to soothe. The hotter one seemed to scald at first, then my body went into a slow release and it felt manageable although over time my head began to feel light. We all stripped down naked and took separate pools.

One pool sat over an edge and I could have easily slipped down off the edge of the cliff. Figures slipped in and out from the trail. I went into the sheltered pool the young woman had chosen to relax in after driving us so far. She left the pool swiftly.

During the next hour, she explained, "In my culture, native culture, it is not right for men and women to be naked around each other after just meeting."

She admitted, "I know you didn't know this, but it made me feel uncomfortable."

I thought to myself, I didn't know about this point. On the other hand, I still did knowingly risk the same body of water as her.

I said, "O, OK, well I get that it made you uncomfortable. I'll try to ask next time I need to be conscious."

I felt glad she had expressed herself. At the same time while I traveled I wanted to be able to express myself unfiltered and act in the moment. When I worked with kids previously there had been strict parameters I had to follow from language to behavior and I didn't want to feel like I was idling anymore as I hitchhiked the country. It felt much better to ask forgiveness if warranted than to ask permission. Also, warranted or not, I felt like I'd apologized to enough women in my life over perceived minor offenses. It seemed to me that they had often taken the victim role, right or wrong, and I'd gotten sick and tired of it. I walked down the hill from whence we came.

Ready to sleep like a log, I slumbered in close to the car. Four hours passed. Crack of awful six or seven something had the young woman waking me up off the dusty ground. She had not slept a wink.

"I wanna get home to my kids."

"Alright."

Wired by motivation, she started driving back the way we came. We could see the smoking charred forest. In broken spots in the woods grey ash contrasted with the still alive green forest.

I didn't mention we had headed back west and north towards Portland away from their northeastern destination. I may have been feeling selfish and that could be why I omitted this fact, but hey we had headed right where I needed to go. If I had redirected the other three to where they wanted it could have easily taken me a day or two longer to get to Portland. As we got closer to Portland, the rest of the crew realized this. I could see the exhaustion in their eyes. They expressed slightly road-weary exasperation at the distance.

We stopped outside of Portland for some random reason so the twenty-year-old could pick up something and talk to his non-related family members. I guessed the relations may have been his more distant foster family though this remained unclear. While he retrieved his things and hung out momentarily with his kin the young woman confided in me.

She said, "Something's going on between us. I like him. I'm not sure of it yet, but I really like him. And I don't know what's going to happen. I don't know how he feels yet."

I could clearly tell they felt close, it was in the way they gave each other affectionate looks. I had surmised this much from the trip so far.

At my request, they dropped me off in downtown Portland. The twenty-year-old good and sentimental gave me a piece of the glass beach. I arrived a few blocks back from the Willamette River just ready to be on my own. I planned to slowly tramp in the direction of Julia's.

One shoe in front of the other in hot Portland, I crossed the bridge. I went to the other side passed the Red Bull Flugtag. I backtracked a few times and checked that I had headed in the right direction. The Flugtag fit Portland well in terms of weird corporate promotions. It's a competition where people try to see how far they can launch their own homemade craft off a ramp and out over the river. Miles later I walked by an elementary school letting out parents, kids, and noise. I stumbled into a bar.

Forcefully I pointed and said to the bartender, "Is this the right way to Southeast?"

The bartender nodded. I guzzled down a couple cold glasses of water and up and onward I went. I rounded the way to her address and loafed through the neighborhood.

"This has to be the house, right?" I said to myself out loud, hoarsely.

I saw a bee mural in the middle of the street and I thought the house must be the one called honey. It had the look of houses I remember from Prescott, Arizona, hippyish, eco-environmentalist. The house felt warm and welcoming, a well lived-in, one story home where bikes regularly journeyed to and from. Still less than one hundred percent sure of the house I texted Julia. I got back that she would be there in an hour. I moseyed about four blocks away. I finally rested on a street bench. I read the local free paper to find out the goings on in the area. Crime in the black community was the only story I found memorable.

Julia called back, excitement was in her voice. She had a light airy welcoming voice almost girlish in its inflection.

I headed over.

She had short hair now, not that she didn't before, but the small dreadlock on the back of her head was gone. Before that one lock had lingered on her neck like a surprise attraction. Her warm glowing smile quickly lit up the room. I saw that she was heavier than before in a healthy way. Her boyfriend made a good cook. I thought back to when Julia and I had both worked for Outward Bound in Philly. After work one day I had drunkenly admitted my interest in her and got rejected.

The three of us rode around the city the next day. The boyfriend tired us out until finally we had Mexican food. Then his friend who volunteered at the theater got us into one of the worst movies of all time, *Amy* about Amy Winehouse.

"It really was no good," I remember saying. Filmed with a home video camera and about nothing deep or important. Though no complaints about the free popcorn and pizza.

Come late morning, we ambled into the park. Julia and I had adorned ourselves with scarves and the like. Kids a playing, a festive atmosphere, we arrived there for the free ice cream. After which looking like dames of an eccentric persuasion, we strolled Madonna-like with a diva attitude into the Museum of Science.

We spoke in fluid, high-society British accents which helped to accentuate our presumptuous diva tone, exclaiming loudly at the many exhibits. We got stuck in the gift shop with Julia's fascination for kid's toys and we ended up relaxing into the light of stars coming down from the screen of the planetarium.

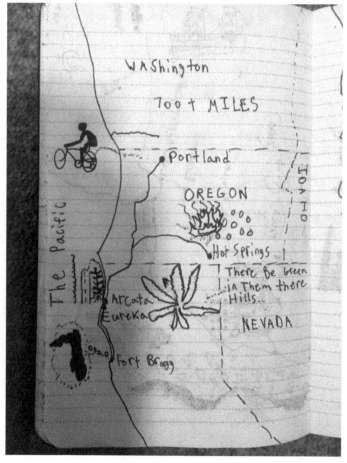

The ride back to Julia's house darkened into night. Next morning rose soon to farewell. I walked out of town with the same old beat up black pack, over the bridge, up the hill through the morning dew of the cemetery and down and up again. I came out of the wiles of nature to a group of shops with a gas station and finally saw a sign to the highway. I got a piece of cardboard from the dumpster. Turned a board into a sign once again. I marked it up, fat sharpie in hand. I observed an on-ramp with multiple roads leading in. Flying the sign away, it didn't take long, I heard someone yelling, "Hey!" Where is it coming from? Left? Right? Back? Ahead? Ahead. A woman with blond curly hair calling from the breakdown lane.

"Hey!" she said again.

She crossed over to the breakdown lane where I stood.

She offered, "Do you want a ride?"

"O yeah! Thanks," I said.

Mid-thirties and into the outdoors I would soon find out. She was headed down to Ashland to get a tattoo and see the theater. Along with her and growing slowly and steadily jealous was her companion. Her protective therapy dog. Definitely the nervous type with a bark, but none too threatening. We talked back and forth, finding things in common and we both poured out past experiences. We had in common, being fellow east coasters exploring out west.

She told me, "I've got one screwed-up alcoholic fuck anything that moves regardless of gender ex."

I listened for a long time.

We stopped and she paid for a beer and food at Ninkasi Brewery in Eugene. After driving for a bit and feeling a little closer I squeezed her leg.

She said, "It hurts. I bruise easily," but she smiled.

We pulled off the road picked up some beers and she talked to the store clerk. She had clearly met him before. We headed nearby to the still hot forest. She parked to show me a spot she liked. The pond looked like more of a dried-out pool with the hard long drought that Oregon had experienced. We sat together while I got hard. She started to have a feel. She looked like she liked what she felt. My eyes looking down, she slipped the trunks down and began to suck. Ahh, it felt good, but only for a short while and not to completion.

She said, "We'll have time to finish this later."

Into Ashland which I expected to be quite pretty, instead the air smelled of smoke and the temperature was hot from ongoing forest fires. Another meal she kindly paid. We sat outside at a restaurant with a back patio and very inexperienced young and of course pretty wait staff. The type of youngness that makes you want a hard-smoking diner working woman in her late 50s. Traveling kids and tourists aplenty in the center of town.

At the hotel, she left me to my own devices as the theater ticked ever closer. Caring less than ever about custom I strode through the hotel just with my trunks and towel in hand.

I arrived at the Jacuzzi. Shortly I got joined by some friendly excitable college-aged kids on their road trip. Sleepy in the hot water I drifted in and out of the conversation.

They invited me back to their rooms to hang and drink.

I said, "Maybe later, I'm waiting for a friend to get back."

Truly tired now I dripped up to the room and took a shower and tried not to touch myself for the sake of later. Hours passed in and out by the TV's light.

Finally, she came back. She had enjoyed the performance thoroughly. Something Shakespearean if memory is at all served.

She took the other bed saying, "You sound tired we can wait to have sex in the morning."

"No."

We curled up in the same bed feeling each other up and down. Her getting on top riding. Me shifting over to doggy style missionary somewhere in there as well. I tried to be somewhat gentle, but I failed as usual even on request. I came in what may have been doggy style with no protection used.

She had told me earlier, "I had cancer and they took my uterus out." Risk of sex with no protection calculated, a casualty to the road, drink, and of course always the most natural feeling. She had not cum claiming that as she got older she did not cum as quickly or commonly with sex as in younger years.

She said, "I don't care as much."

I did not believe this self-delusional bullshit for a second.

After I came a big spot appeared in the middle of the sheets. She said, "You can have this bed," slipping into the other.

I halfheartedly complained relenting in the end with a tired smile. I lay down to the side of the spot. Her in her bed, me in ours. Hunger sated for the moment.

Early morning darkness still cloaked the room. Again my own urge grew, feeling back and forth as we had before. Maybe my actions had a porn influence which at least she had some familiarity with. I directed her to go down to the carpet both of us fully naked. Directing her down as I stood, on her knees she began licking and sucking. Just as she started to get uncomfortable with this I reached my long right arm down finger pressed against her vulva up in towards the clitoris. Her discomfort visibly started to diminish eyes changing in the dark dim light. She started to get wetter. Back to the bed, now positioned on the edge. From her mouth, I tried in the timeliest way to slip it inside keeping the tension. Back and forth. She seemed to be getting there.

I told her, "I'm gonna cum."

Right after I had, she had not and again did not seem to be bothered. The time for the classic hotel breakfast with weird tasting orange juice had arrived. She seemed up for it. I had tired groggy as hell bleary eyes and disliked the idea of conversation over the breakfast buffet.

I gathered my belongings, the time to hit the road once again had come. She asked with her blue eyes looking across at me if I wanted to exchange phone numbers as she had decided to move east back to New Hampshire.

I said "No," thinking it unrealistic.

Hugged and kissed her goodbye, saying "It was fun," and the normal "take care of yourself."

She could see I felt ready to travel on. And off I went to the gas station and over the bridge to the on-ramp.

There stood a young thru-hiker of the Pacific Crest Trail. He hung out down from where the sidewalk crosses the on-ramp.

Out materialized a street guy from a shelter down the on-ramp.

He said, "This is the spot to be picked up!"

Quickly lumbering in came a black SUV with a lumbering behemoth to match inside.

He said, "Y'a gonna hop in!"

I got in, so did the hiker as I offered him a beer which he turned down. The hiker got dropped off quickly down the road. In turn, I got left in shotgun with the big ole boy hardcore rap blasting out the speakers.

A good ole Indiana boy. Although when he revealed more, the good part of him many would question from a moral standpoint. especially those from the place he hailed.

Flying downhill, erratic driving into California he told me,

"I'm coming from Portland and I've been seeing this girl. She's in her early 20s."

He showed me on his phone a standard body shot tatts, fake boobs and all.

"She's a stripper."

I thought, *of course she's a stripper.*

"I've been paying for her even when I go back home to my wife and kids in Indiana. She's stopped stripping for me. It's costing me a fair bit of cash, but hey the young pussy is making me happy."

"If you can pay for it..." I said mischievously and slightly sarcastically.

Indiana said, "I had to put my wife in line when we weren't having sex often enough. Now we have it at least four times a week."

Pleased to be on the West Coast he repeatedly pulled out his mostly cached pipe and puffed the remnants of the weed that may or may not still have been there. I talked, mostly just playing along. I had just gotten out of bed with a woman and now I headed to see Shay down in Oakland.

"Yeah well I'm a piece of shit, I know it. Hey, she makes me happy though," sweating in the heat and furrowing his brow.

We continued downhill then saw speed lights flashing

behind us, the cops had picked us up. Pulling over more annoyed than scared, somehow still somewhat jolly, he acted over- amiably as he shuffled through looking for his license and registration. We got told to get out of the vehicle.

Indiana agreed, "Sure thing." He nodded his head up and down.

The cops said, "Can we search your vehicle."

Indiana said, "O yeah."

To my disappointment, he agreed almost enthusiastically to having his car searched which meant that they would definitely want to search my bag as well. Nothing too problematic had found itself into my bag this time. I just wished he hadn't voided his rights so quickly. It would be unproductive for travel, but just once it would have pleased me to see the subtext 'You can fuck off' thrown into the mix.

The cops said, "Can we see some ID?"

Checking our IDs both cops' eyebrows raised. One from Massachusetts one from Indiana and the plate from out west mismatched both of our licenses. The mismatch definitely failed to work in our favor. Also both of us taller than the cops. As a California cop when he came across the weed pipe he didn't care too much. I thought this act was at least refreshing. Most other states in the country we could have easily gotten done for the pipe. California at least had seen a crack of light through the federal government's drug war with medical marijuana legalized and possession down to a citation-worthy offense. Low amounts of possession were mostly deprioritized by local police departments. He searched and searched through the SUV with its myriad of luggage falling out the back and other comfort items askew. His partner and I eyed each other up and down as the tension grew. I tried to de-escalate it a little still staring back and forth with him while making both my hands clearly visible. The hot day strained the situation further. The first cop continued to rifle through. Then he moved up to the dash bringing his tool with him. It looked like a screwdriver with an L in it. A lever of sorts. He started pulling back the vents and cracked one a little bit.

Seeing this, Indiana started gesticulating. going up to the cop telling him loudly,

"You broke it, you broke it!"

Cop flatly, "No I didn't."

"Yeah, you did!"

The cop a little sheepishly ended up letting us off with a warning.

Indiana said once we had gotten safely back in the car and somewhat out of earshot,   "Fucking mother fucking idiots!"

Indiana on the phone now, "Hey! I picked up a hitchhiker," to the stripper gal.

She responded by saying something about how he acted crazy and she found this displeasing. He had a gleam in his eye when he talked to her.

How is it different, the morality of summer? Relationships, liaisons, things open up. The opposite season, winter, is closed down, only what's necessary. Fall grabbing, grasping on. Spring maybe something can happen.

He dropped me outside of Sacramento and I flashed my sign for a ride, but damn it! I had a show to get to that night. Tre Fuck also known as Trevor's show. I ended up walking into the nearby hotel and getting the number for a cab. Telling the cab to meet me outside of the Burger King looking bedraggled as ever. The Indian cab driver pulled up demanding immediate payment looking back at me.

"Alright, Alright, Alright" pulling out a twenty he started to relax.

He relaxed further as we talked, back and forth. Tipping him his eyes lightened, his brow smoothed and he actually looked happy at the end of the ride to the Greyhound station. His tough shift had almost ended and the sun peered through his window as thoughts of home seemed to percolate in his head. In and out of consciousness seeing the bay appear on the ride, sun setting, time a wasting. A few interchanges of muni train later and I had arrived in northwestern San Fran. I headed to the show venue. Unfortunately, I had just missed Trevor's band TSA play. They have incredibly short punk sets with each song registering under a minute in length. When I asked why his band is called TSA, Trevor said it had no special meaning. Although with a touch of humor he added TSA could stand for Thinly Sliced Avocado, TyrannoSaurus Ass, Trevor Sucks Ass or The Starving Artist. We ended up rocking out and him a small guy ping-ponging back and forth constant energy in the room. The music felt good, but coming from the East Coast Boston scene and hanging with bands in Arizona and Sonora, I saw it as disgusting how fucking polite these San Francisco punks acted. Also the bands a little uptight at some crass bravado.

After, I headed back to Trevor's place where he, his brother and girlfriend and another friend lived. The apartment building inhabited a position close to the ocean. Being back in San Fran we of course drank and got really high on some fine bud. His brother worked late night security and the girlfriend came out to hang in only her bathrobe. She approached us very sexy as only a Belarusian woman can be and her weirdness made her more so. At this point in the haze, memory starts to fail.

I knew Trevor from when I went to Prescott College. We shared a close friend, my buddy Matteo, who now lived down in New Mexico. Together with a guy named Mike they had formed a hip-hop group named Knockout Rock that would occasionally perform around town. More than performing they liked to hang out and spit rhymes to each other. Trevor would mix up beats and all three would rhyme over them. He got fed up with Prescott College and headed back to San Fran. I had last seen him a few years earlier with equally hazy memory on 4/20.

His brother got back come morning and we smoked again with Tre's roommate and she kindly looked up the places I wanted to go on her phone. I set out to San Francisco State University where Tre Fuck had given me his ID and password and got some online errands done. Afterward, I met up with him saying goodbye and we split on the way up the hill. I walked and walked finding a bookshop with Karl Ove Knausgård's six-volume *My Struggle* or *Mein Kampf,* massive in its size, a true saga of the painful daily life he has led. Told with ferocious honesty that would upset his family deeply. This is the type of unbridled truth telling I've long admired.

Looking for a map I found a couple made by AAA to head south with. The maps overall looked useful though more precision could have helped. Next a charger, and as silly as I felt buying the charger with an unnecessary phone it still ended up being cheaper than buying a charger alone. Talking to the salesman he wished he could be doing some of the travel I had engaged in. And so I sat Oh so accomplished, as light darkened over the library in the city across the bay with beauty, and cold wetness arriving at warmer Oakland, Shay back on the mind.

Tip: Be aware of your own location and use your own judgment not necessarily the driver's when you have the option of where to be dropped off.

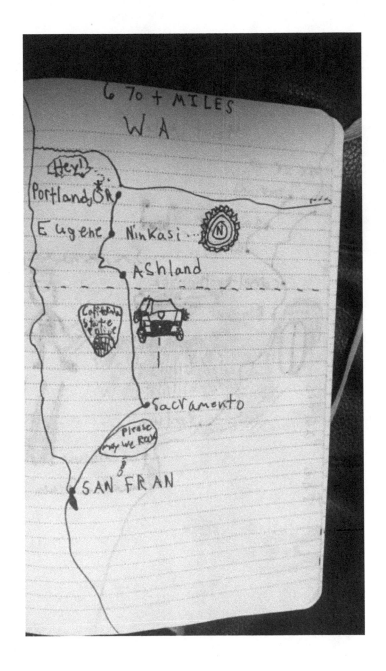

Chapter 11

She had been camped out in her room, back in hermit mode for the last week after having enough of the partying that comes with life as a bartender. She was fed up with customers and looked forward to getting her hosting gig more fully off the ground in San Fran. It was a hike up the hill and she met me outside, cigarette in her hand.

She told me, "I'm sick of these fucking customers. You know I've been bartending for years now." Soon she was smoking away sitting down back from the sidewalk looking up at a few stars visible up the hill and over the street lamp.

We headed in. In her apartment, she had her bong, cast aside laptop perched on her belly. She wanted a slow night to zone out so she stared into the screen to sleep. I was horny and looking for action after being on the road. The other woman I had been with faded in and out of my consciousness. The night at the river where she went off to sleep in a hammock probably played in my subconscious not helping. My travels played their own part not helping her feelings of insecurity. So we tried to go to sleep, but come the wee hours of the morning I tried to get things going with my cock constantly pressing up against her backside kisses creeping up her arm, but no she wanted to sleep. My hand drifted down betwixt her legs more mischievously than sexually, I was no longer hard. Her reaction was strong,

"Why don't you just do it then! Do it!" pulling down her boxers showing her bare ass.

I recoiled surprised and disgusted.

"Not like this, not like this," getting serious the second time round in a monotone shaking my head.

She said, "You don't feel genuine," and quickly ran to the bathroom closing the door.

Taking this in for a split second, I jumped up trundling to the bathroom door roaring,

"We're gonna talk about this."

After a time in the bathroom, she went into the living room and lay down to sleep. Tension still in the air, but it was quiet, real quiet with the sun drifting through the shades of the apartment on the hill. I dressed gathering my things quickly. It was time to go. I went over to her making sure she was covered by a blanket whispering,

"We'll talk about this later."

Leaving the apartment, down the bit of grass near the bus stop, to the sidewalk of the main numbered street, the morning light glared horribly into my eyes. I called my cousin, "I was just wondering if I could stop by for a few hours?"

All I wanted was to see if I could steal a few hours to get my shit together at her apartment. I could hear the unease and frustration in her voice no doubt related to her relationship with Rosie continuing to slowly get rockier and rockier.

She said, No, they were both out.

I walked around Lake Merritt thoughts streaming through my mind. I sat down under a tree the grass damp. Feeling frustrated, lonely and alone in yet another city by another name. I read Karl Ove Knausgård's *My Struggle* over the next two hours, lines from the book crackling through under my eyes and over my brow, cold underneath the arms reaching into the body and forehead, sweating through the bandanna tied tightly back, stopping the heavy wild hair from covering my sad eyes.

"The only thing I have learned from life is to endure it," Knausgård writes.

It was time to make some forward movement and to be distracted by one of the most basic goals. I was hungry and went to a local café where I got a worthwhile hot chocolate and pastry slowly stirring the spirits. The price? It is in the Bay, so something silly and too much for this traveler's slowly depreciating budget. Reading my book an old man sat nearby reading his newspaper. I glanced over at him doing his own routine. It helped and I started to feel more part of the society I had been traveling through and less an outsider on the edge. I started to collect my thoughts and went back to my spot at Lake Merritt thinking of my next move. I laid down to rest and plan.

On the road, you can drop down and rise up so easily.

Shay texted me saying I should stop by the bar before I leave. I thought of what to say repeating it in my mind.

She offered, "Would you like a drink?"

"No, I'm good," I said.

It would have been a Guinness. As she came over her blue eyes looked at me across the bar. Tiredness in my voice, "Our communication is horrible."

She agreed, we talked just a few sentences more and hugged and kissed goodbye. Sent a text to her much later that said let's talk after you come back from France, after the Burn. There was no response. That's fine. Though if I had told the unbridled truth in full when we were both lying on the bed together would the response have changed?

I do feel differently now. Yes, I do feel horny. Yes, maybe I'm somewhat distracted.

I saw another woman on the road. She picked me up. We hooked up.

My sole focus isn't on you. I still want you.

That poster on your wall gives me doubts. That half-naked woman raises questions for me about your sexuality. Where are you at, with who you're attracted to?

Cuz, where I'm at is I'm gonna keep on moving, unless, and this is a giant unless, there is something else.

So let me know if there is. If there is then we can figure something out now or at least plan for later. If not though just make it clear, tell me.

Because I'm out on the road with nowhere to go but south. Chances are I'll be laying my head down on my mat in the ditch by the off-ramp.

So I need to know.

What do you want?

What do you need?

And that is the double-edged sword whereas her initial attraction may have had to do with my ramblings so did her justified feelings of insecurity at my leaving town only to return two random weeks later.

The price of relationships made through travel? Ahh, but does it make things more dynamic? Are you then an exotic commodity? What would or wouldn't happen if you stayed?

I took rides then got on a train to San Jose. In talking to the station attendant I figured out which bus would take me further south. I walked around outside the station and spotted a traveler kid. I observed how he hit up people for money at the station. He would sit down with his sign and flash it up at them. He was still young enough that people would think he was cute and give him money to warm their hearts. I went off and got a few beers and some food at a restaurant bar with a band jamming up front sating the mind. I sat down at the bus stop next to a guy in his forties and at this point, it was a comic ego boost to be hit on, but I showed I was not interested in the slightest and continued to indulge his eccentricity. The bus finally came and south I went to another inland California town by the name of Gilroy. The bus arrived really late and the crime looked higher in this town with its rough surroundings of corner stores and bad paint jobs. I walked around picked up my basic fixings here and there. Sleep was not the easiest to come by. Come late morning I found that the bus with the best destination was Carmel-by-the-Sea and at this rate, I would be back on Route 1, much better for hitching and prettier too. As I stood, a woman who looked like a tranny with a chubbed-out gut started to talk to me,

"My pussy, My pussy it feels so good."

She went on and on repeating herself dressed in black her hands stuck in her pockets, lipstick smeared. Once again with a disinterested look I made sure she knew I was not interested.

At this point on the road, she had become a novelty, a moment of entertainment with my mind going "Ehh, alright, who's gonna happen next?" Her offer unlike so many was direct and I had much respect for the clarity. She was moaning about trying to get further down the road to

"Salinas, Salinaaas."

The bus rolled in. The woman split. Thankful for this respite I hopped on and the bus rolled into Carmel-by-the-Sea and it was still morning.

Capitalism in the teeth. Broken people, but who are they? The ones looking in or out on the street?

The air was fresh there were travelers around in town, but for me, it was time to hitch southward to make the most of the day. The first ride was from a really nice taxi driver who was short on clients at the moment and brought me down a little way until I was directed towards the road to Big Sur. And then one of the better rides of the trip from this wealthy gay Latin artist who grew up poor and now owned houses in California, Florida and outside the country.

"In Florida, I have friends who just housesit for me and all that I ask is they take care of the home and when I come to Florida they leave the house and let me be."

He asked me, "Why are you traveling?"

"Right now I'm heading to see my friend Ra in LA. In general for the adventure."

"People used to hitch more back in the 70s and it was fine, but when Reagan closed down all of the mental hospitals it got desperate. I had a guy I picked up try to steal my convertible. The alarm system I have locked him in and he was still inside when the cops came around."

He drove me back to his house and asked if I wanted a beer and a shower. I said no to the shower, but took the beer. His place was classy with marble. It was modern Californian and had a view out toward the ocean.

He explained himself, "Yeah at this point I've got this money and I pretty much have paid my family to stay away from me."

It seems they were not too happy with him being gay. Though with his friendly nature he now had friends all over the place and a lover who was currently out of the country.

Off we went back into the convertible and back to the highway where the sun was shining down on the big blue Pacific. Before getting out of the car he gave me a few dollars and said,

"I like you, you're traveling for the right reason."

He had spotted a dusty guy and gal waiting on the other side of the road and was heading back to pick them up.

Manhood, a rite of passage, does it equal meaning? Proving yourself to yourself. To set a goal and follow thru.

Dirt sides of the road trampled with mirth as visions of hope play in the eyes of those who have tread this path, years upon years have made their mark, the kind feet of Big Sur. Influenced to come through here by my father. He was no stranger to wanderlust whether it be travel or the heart. He had suggested a place by the name of Esalen. A place of ideas and writers stretching back to the fifties. Seeing the trees the coast nearby the calming nature even with the whizzing of cars going by, the location of the retreat seemed plain as day.

Riding along the cliffs of the 1, a surfer in the driver's seat, bedraggled traveler the passenger, car made for scouting the waves west side of the road, the drop, down below expanding outward into sunshiny blue. He had been out looking for waves and we stopped to look out to see if there were any to be caught. Views abounded off the right side, sealions sunning themselves tusks out outstretched like potatoes slowly baking being stared at by floral tourists with glee.

A young guy slightly taller than me, short hair looking like a prototypical Cali surfer; blond, young, muscular, thin not too thin, looking for adventure, a car of his own, a perfect commercial for the state. He had even designed his car with compartments for practical use. The compartments were made out of wood the same hue as balsa that looked smooth to the touch.

Opening the compartments, "I built them myself. I can put tools in here and camping gear over here."

He pointed to the different compartments beaming a proud smile.

I was definitely a bit jealous wanting the lifestyle at the same time glad that I had finished college and I was at a different place in my life. All I could say repeatedly was "Cool" when he showed me.

We stopped by an In-N-Out and picked up double doubles as we headed to Ventura. He played a new track from the young beginning to be famous MC "Joey Badass." He was pleased to have a random character up for fun, but alas his friend's beach house was not to be. I was dropped off at a gas station and hopped the fence of a house that had a long walkway up to the hill and slept in the backyard.

In the morning I found out that there was a bus station a couple of miles walk away, and with that, and another more direct bus ride I made it into the LA bus station. I called Ra upon arriving.

He told me, "Catch the train out to Crenshaw. Make sure you get off at the right stop. Some of those train stops drop you off in a tougher area. I don't want you getting in trouble."

I arrived and there was a massive cathedral right off the stop that a lot of money had been put into. It had been more than two years since we had seen each other. He had been one of my major intellectual influences while at college and a cause for sanity. One of the more comic memories I have is the two of us walking into the Prescott Supermarket Fry's. Both over six feet tall and not the most common looking type of guys for the area. Ra with a large hat presumably holding massive locks inside. Me the wild mountain man with long dreaded hair. Both of us sporting beards and backpacks and clearly not from Prescott originally. To say we drew eyes would be an understatement. It was more noticeable when the two of us were together there, but being stared at in public was not uncommon for either one of us.

Another memory is Ra holding up his newborn son Kaleel at graduation like Simba from *The Lion King*. It was no surprise that when I did meet his son they had worked out a Lion's nickname between the two of them. He pulled up and we went to the first Starbucks that I had ever been to where almost everybody was black. Inside on the poster board different community events were posted. While this was new to me I still tend to hate coffee shops in general especially chain ones. It's got something to do with people pontificating combined with stimulants, electronics, anxiety, and too much energy trapped inside. Basically, a disgusting form of reserved repressed conformed intellectualism. Add in a dose of physical inaction and (not in this case, but often enough) abhorrent judgmental self-righteousness. I left right away.

Anyway went to a market that had African items, dancing, a drum circle, and food. It seemed a place that was the real heart of the local community. Kids played on the pavement to the side of the market, families gathered, people intermingling in the heat of the day. Ra asked if I wanted to get food here, but I said I would get it later, Mexican would be on the menu.

Ra debated out loud, "I kinda wanna take you, but I don't know if I should take you over to the Watts Towers. If you were a regular white guy it wouldn't be a problem. A white guy with dreads might piss people off."

We got out of the car and Ra nodded and greeted a couple of tougher looking guys walking by with a "word." The "word" greeting, male toughness, you alright, I'm alright. Toughness OK? OK was needed to say, I can pass you? You can pass. I belong here. It also seemed to me that Ra did not feel safe in this area. I knew nothing about the towers but read the placards around the towers as Ra explained. This Italian guy named Sam Rodia who had left a relationship and possibly a family behind devoted years of his life to this vision. He slowly built these towers out of concrete so that they would be structurally sound. Now it had become a community mosaic where volunteers would get together and fix the towers. Ra liked Rodia for his sheer madness and his pursuit of this ideal. It was an idea, not meant to bring him wealth, or fame, or admiration, but was purely about seeing a personal vision realized. What makes this vision starker is that it is in Watts, a poorer place that has seen much strife extending well into the present. Throughout the time we were there it was relatively quiet, but there was a wariness about the place. I had not expected that the area around the towers would be mixed, but it was: some houses with black residents and others with Mexican or Central American inhabitants.

We got back in the car and Ra went to pick up Kaleel at daycare. He had a beaming smile, and with Ra as his father, he exuded intelligence.

"Of course," Ra said. "All the teachers love him".

He was an active child, Ra introduced me and he was so happy to see his dad. Not surprisingly highly verbal he asked questions and talked away looking outward seemingly interested in taking in as much information as possible. Ra dropped off Kaleel and it was good to see him in a different role than I had witnessed before. As a father, he encouraged Kaleel, pushing him when necessary, joking as well, and was stern with him when needed.

Ra's father had died in the last few years and he had been a secretive guy. Upon his death, family secrets were revealed and I think it had sent Ra for a little mental tailspin about his own view on his father and the family. This mind bend may also have been due to the fact that at Prescott College Ra got deep into studying family systems theory.

My own mind reflected back on my differing relationship with my father who I had met as an adult. Ra and I are very different people, but women definitely played the larger role in terms of the time involved raising us. Ra tended to like to hang out more with women. Because I had two female parents, I went the other way while growing up and mainly had guy friends. As a whole, though, guys tended to bore me more easily. The sexual attraction was not there. Also, being a guy myself I found most guys predictable and banal.

The original Mexican restaurant Ra had wanted to show me was holding a family event so we went to another one and then he made sure to drop me off at a knockoff travel lodge that he had stayed at before. He looked out to make sure that I got a safe hotel room when I suggested that I was used to finding a place to crash outside. He may have last been at this hotel as a teenager, years ago. When I was dropped off, I went in to get a room and behind me was a tall voluptuous black woman. Communication with the manager and possible owner of the hotel was difficult and he was already in a crap mood, the lines furrowed across his forehead after years of stress. He was clearly from India with his strong accent. Hearing that the woman behind me wanted nonsmoking I suggested to him that we could simply switch rooms. At this, his temper grew,

"So you don't want the room, so you don't want the room?"

"No, no, I was seeing if we could switch the rooms."

"So you don't want the room, so you don't want the room? Next! Next!"

Fuckin hell guy, really!

"No, I want the room. I'll keep the room."

I paid, trying to show calm on my face while inside frustration grew along with apprehension, thinking that it was unlikely I would find another half-decent place not outrageously priced in the area. Quietly I still offered to help the woman with her bags after she had paid. She accepted with a slow smile. The owner looked like he had been fucked with many a time in this neighborhood and had lost perspective and the ability to listen. I left keys in hand and dropped my stuff off at the room, coming back out as she pulled around. I waited for the guy to leave his post at the thick glass inside. Her white car was full of luggage which she was having some trouble getting up. I picked it up and brought it in.

Inside the room smoky with her many colored bags lying about, leopard-print not far from the eye. She was sitting on the edge of the bed, long hair hanging down over the shoulders. My tired eyes looked back. Talking slowly back and forth,

"We could hang out in your room. I've got drugs," she said drawing it out.

Doubting my ability to stay awake and having little willingness to partake in hanging out with yet another person,

"Nah tonight I think I'm just gonna rest up."

Then I closed the door slowly and made my way downstairs to relax and watch aimless premium television, a luxury induced hypnosis. We shared our aloneness; her with her hotel room, me with mine. Her with her many bags and drugs, me with the TV that had HBO. Two people passing through a rougher side of LA, alone in common.

Ra picked me up the next morning as I was racing around on the block outside the hotel getting a morning snack from one of the shoddy convenience stores. The heat was already starting to pick up in South Central. We stopped at a nearby gas station and I told him about the woman. He said he would have... raising his eyes.

"The one thing is I'm not sure if she was a tranny or not. The light was dim and she was a bigger woman with trimmed eyebrows and long straight hair."

In response, Ra said, "I would know."

"Really, there are pretty good-looking trannies out there."

"Naw, I would know, you can tell the difference."

"Fair enough."

Not in agreement on whether or not you can clearly identify a transsexual just by looking, we headed to the park and walked over to the edge near a metal fence.

"Do you want to be in the sun or the shade," asked Ra.

"The sun."

Ra waxed philosophical over so many subjects winding them together, from the political, to the scientific, to the familial and otherwise. As usual, I would keep up with him for a bit, but he would always make jumps with a wit that would leave me mentally dragging behind. He had a special little tool for rolling his weed that I had never seen before and the blunt certainly helped loosen up our talking. Thinking back now this whole section of time was done with much ceremony. While the weed opened the conversation it did make quick access to memory a bit harder. Ra had been wanting to go to grad school at UCLA where I'm sure he would take to it like a fish to water given the academic environment. I asked about him wanting to start a school and he had talked to some people, but money was again the issue. He did miss living in quieter Prescott as well as the focused study and discussion of ideas to be explored, not that I think he would have opted for a trade.

It was getting hotter in the park and a single line of sweat was coming down from Ra's hat. We slowly got up to leave the relatively quieter city park and it was time for food. I looked back over towards the green, the land shaded by trees, kids jubilantly ran around playing on the playground. Ra drove pumping a range of music with warm beats and the next song unpredictable from the last. The freeway grew hotter as we sped along into downtown LA traffic. It had been a while since last I was in a friend's personal car and a few random memories of other times years ago briefly brimmed into view. One of them my friend Whitney in her car as the sun set in bright polluted colors loving LA for the reasons many an east coaster hated it. She was back in Connecticut now saving money living with family wishing she was back out here involved in the music industry.

We arrived at the small Peruvian restaurant that was bustling with people. I tried to hold my own a bit with Ra as gluttonous portions of barbecue and other delicious Peruvian food was ordered. I thoroughly enjoyed sitting there with Ra chowing down devouring as much as possible with the wide range of exotic sauces setting off the variety of food. The kitchen was small and crammed in right near the seats and Spanish was spoken rapidly. It would slow down when a familiar face arrived and a more laid-back casual conversation would take place. We left slowly weighted down by the leftovers in our hands and the dinner Ra had specifically ordered for later.

"Do you still want to go to the beach?"

I did and advocated it. There was a beach close to his, but we went to Manhattan which was a little more upscale and scenic. I had forgotten that I stayed the night there while going to Prescott. A friend of my former roommate named Will grew up there who had the look of a well-off Cali beach guy. Time was a wasting and Ra said he needed to get back to Crenshaw, "You've got ten minutes." I quickly ran down to the beach as the meter police were not far off. Dove in did a few strokes and started rushing back messily and sandily slipping into my black jeans. Forced my shoes on and ran back up the hill where the car was parked. I got back out of breadth and Ra was around the corner on the phone. He looked more relaxed than ten minutes before, either the call or just being by the beach had an effect. I didn't ask and it was impossible to discern. He dropped me off at the same train station that we'd met at, said our see ya laters and the night's journey to Fullerton started. His mischievous playful half-smile with one eye raised comes through vividly even today.

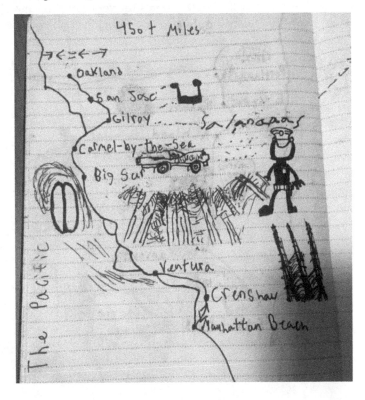

I was on my way to the one grandiose luxury of the trip. The one cloth I had looked up and caught my eye with the utmost flash and pizzazz. Staring out at me from a computer screen thousands of miles away I knew I had to get one. I couldn't just order it this was something that had to be done in person and I had called ahead to make sure they were open and could see me.

Downtown, a beer just before the bus, bent head coming out of a darkly lit LA bar more relaxed than perfectly sober with sore backpack strap shoulders. One bus, then another bus late into the night and I arrived in Fullerton where I set up camp on a hill next to a bridge for the train and above the main road. Beneath that led to the highway. Morning came I was sitting hanging out on the benches, bagel and cream cheese messily in hand. I walked back towards the zoot suit shop and found a small abandoned parking lot to rest behind the wall. El Chapuco Zoot Suits would not be open for the next couple of hours. I waited for my appointment with the red devil.

When the time came I walked in and introduced myself to the mother and daughter who ran the store. There was another man being fitted for his zoot suit he was renting to take to a wedding. The store had been around since 1978 and was inspired by a play called "Zoot Suit." El Chapuco was the main character. While I was being fitted and checking on prices for the different parts of the suit occasional facts were dropped about the store and the zoot suit, but with my focus solely on the red devil, they quickly flew away. The women expressed warmth and care for their family store. The one part of the suit I refused to get was the tie. With a beard undergirding your chin, a tie feels even more claustrophobic than usual. When eating it is always problematic, and my objection runs right down from my grandfather, who after working in New York City for much of his life, never wore a tie again once he had he retired. At a family wedding when I was thirteen and getting edged in the direction of "appropriate formal attire," he and I were the only ones who remained tie-less. Him with his Guayabera and me in a dress shirt. The woman fit the suit well and I came back two hours later once adjustments had been made. Looking in the mirror, red devil to the nines, gleam in one eye, a smirk creeping out from the lower right side of my lips, I was more than pleased at the western hustler reflected back.

Paying the hundreds of dollars sum for the suit as well as the hat and shoes, I thanked them deeply and wished them well. Off I went suit bag strapped on to my dirty backpack, hat attached to it, too. I caught a bus heading east to the desert and the palms.

Transportation intermingling with hitching, I had gone off the I-10 to Route 62 and ended up in the Morongo Valley with a guy who was working construction through the area. He had been through his share of a messy relationship. Restraining orders a recent memory. We stopped at a convenience store where the mood was verging on hostile seeing us coming in. Not more than ten words were spoken. The store had been robbed recently and they had their guard up. The valley was very hit and miss people wise. Some open some closed off. There was a base and testing area nearby and many vets lived in the area. Before leaving his car the working man said,

"I gotta show ya a couple of card tricks."

"Alright," I replied, interested though still somewhat hesitant.

He reached over and took a pack of cards out showing me the tricks on the now hot dusty middle seat. Although I tried to remember I could not seem to come up with the important one or two details that made the trick work later on. Excited about what he had just shared,

"It might help ya to get by."

I thanked him and was left out into the hot desert sun getting steadily closer to nowhere. A friendly middle-aged gentleman gave a ride up the hill to the bus station. On the bus, there were characters aplenty who knew each other on a weekly basis. Most were older and a couple would playfully chat up their frequent acquaintances. Walmart and the medical facilities were the two most common stop-off points. One guy was telling his plight to the front of the bus he hoped his family would pick him up with his car after he got through his ordeal dealing with an ailment and all it entailed. People hailed from close and far, but most had a tough desert rat sense of humor only unfamiliar to me to the extent that it was Californian rather than Arizonan. At some point, we passed by J-Tree as the climbers I've known who love it call it. On this day I pictured the rock burning a hand as a rock jock extended for his first hold at Joshua Tree.

One of the stops to my amusement and the lady driver's obvious abhorrence was the Tortoise Rock Casino. I looked around, but they had closed out all of the roulette tables for the moment. Talking to a casino employee and getting some free casino credit fades in and out of memory, but just after I sat down at a table to put my meager lunch together a guy who had won a little bit dropped a few bills my way. Seeing this, my energy was back up from the bus ride and I was pleased to be walking on down to the Twenty-Nine Palms post office. I phoned back reaching the ladies (my mother's) at home and I had (my father) Anthony's address in hand to send him Karl Ove Knausgård's first book of *My Struggle*. It seemed fitting and I was pleased with the connection to my father and his love for literature. After a moment of sweating in the cool air-conditioned post office, I paid and sent the book on its way.

I waited and waited in the hot sun of Route 62. Cars passed. An older guy on his bicycle went by. Still nothing. Shaded my head with my cardboard sign. Nobody… Then an ex-military guy in his pickup truck, crew cut hair and all, picked me up agreeing to drive "… lil ways into the desert."

He had lived here when he was active out this way and after a time he had returned making it his home. He dropped me off in something less than a ghost village. There was an abandoned looking shop I took shade under. Across the road the shell of a military vehicle stated what this place was about, damn if it didn't look abandoned as well. No cars came for a time. Then an eighteen-wheeler rolled by and a few more cars going the wrong way. I tasted the last few drops of water in the bottle and then it was empty. And no not regular empty it was empty empty, desert empty. The type of empty where something dries and is ready to crack. At a certain point mirages of floating dust took up space on the horizon line.

How can you live a life minimizing risk?

Death around the corner, but it never arrives. How safe are you in your everyday life? How really safe are you? Car accidents. You can die on the toilet, at your child's Little League or soccer game. Drop dead coronary, high cholesterol.

Really it hadn't been that long forty minutes an hour and a half, but in the summer desert that's more than enough time to be exposed and start to feel loopy in the Mojave. Sitting in that, in that sand, life was quickly evaporating out of my body into the utter dryness. I looked up and saw a small compact was coming and I got up real slow heart beating and flagged him down. It was a middle-aged man alone. He had adult sons elsewhere and a dead wife. He was out this way to take care of his parents. He had a friendly little dog and he was always learning. I thanked him profusely as my cracked lips and red scalp took a break from the light overhead. He talked openly about his life and relationships with his sons and parents and wife. I told him of the guy who showed me the card trick. In agreement he said,

"If you're just willing to listen and take the time you can learn so many things in this life."

The sun was setting as the traveler bid farewell to another kind transport. Water was to be had at the spigot from the one shop at Vidal Junction. The road kept going to Parker. It was time to settle in as the same beans were eaten again. Time moved on, the desert cooled minimally. The stars came out and I gazed up at the brightness as eighteen-wheelers rolled in and out shining their light on the scrubland.

Tip: If the person minding a register is nervous and you need to ask them a question: Be direct and succinct. Get in get out go on your way with purpose. You don't need a headache.

Chapter 12

Morning came and I was up with the sun knowing the heat would come with it. I took a left around the corner now aiming for Needles. More eighteen-wheelers rolled by and they dusted up my lungs with a cough. Military vehicles stopped off resting and getting their cargo and caravan line in order. Not wanting to wait around longer even though the likelihood was low, I went over to five of the military guys and saw if a ride was possible. They looked over and gave the likely answer,

"No it's military, blah, blah, it's not up to them."

Vidal, junction of Route 95 and Route 62.

Then she came, the young evangelist close in age to me. Her hoop-D speakers playing Christian stadium rock and other Christian modern tunes. She had a few janky teeth on one side of her mouth, this did not disguise her prettiness which was magnified by her caring spirit. The church she was a part of was definitely a modern one.

It sparked my interest when she said, "We have a booth at a porn convention in Vegas. We can't be too preachy, we engage them in conversation then if they're interested we tell them more about our church and try to help them because they're looking for guidance."

They did this undercover taking people in, then giving their real spiel. She talked of her coworker who put people off by her aggressive approach with the word of the Lord. On other hand my driver had seen more tides of life. A giving person who was off to teach religious classes to kids. A talented golfer who then had a calling. Golf still in the mind if it was with the

Lord's will. She had been raped, survived, and now was happy, had left her hate behind. From this, she was far less judgmental than I expected.

Then I was left by the I-40 in Needles, pleased to have met her, but happy to be out of the car with its religious totality, something I have no desire for in my day-to-day life. The rough around the edges southwest was close. And this concrete well alive atheist was ready for the Wild West once again.

Throughout the journey people's views were projected onto me. Their own past trips, hitching when they were young wild 'n' loose Rob and Michael coming to mind. Drivers would tell me things they wouldn't tell their families, that big ole Indiana boy with his mistress. Or their own children in the case of the father who saved me from heat and dehydration. My cousin and her husband, who had had his own raucous times in LA when he was young, looked at my trip in relation to their daughter now. And most recently the young woman was citing a subtext of a religious journey, Jesus and a biblical narrative echoing in the foreground.

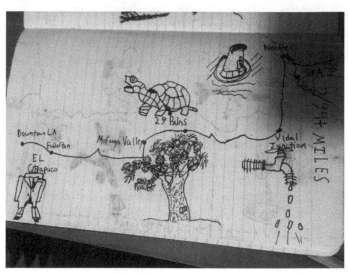

Free and relieved, I hopped into a pickup headed to Kingman, air hitting my face as a big goofy smile opened up in the wind. My accompanying hat for the zoot suit was left in the dust along the guardrail. Annoyance flitted through my mind at my forgetfulness. It was only momentary and better saved for a time in the future, not when pleasure at seeing the red rocks of Arizona was so near.

After resting for a short time at the Kingman gas station and being reminded that Arizona has the nicest convenience stores in all the country I waited along the on-ramp. The pickup was from a Japanese father and son who spoke very little English. They were typical tourists except more adventurous. The father had been drinking away and gambling the night before up in Vegas. There was a lot of motioning and using hands to describe things. They dropped me off in Seligman, but not finding what they wanted swung back around within fifteen minutes and picked me back up. They had gotten an advertisement for a Wild West Show. The only problem was that the location for the show was nondescript. It being Arizona there was also more than one Wild West Show along this stretch of the I-40. I tried to help them figure it out while the father drove as if it was his sole duty. We made it to Ash Fork and I talked to the older clerk at the gas station.

She said, "It happens right here in town at seven."

I communicated this to the guys and saw them one last time as they drove by. Who knows if they ever made it to the show or just headed the way the sign was pointing, to the Grand Canyon?

The down ramp, as I saw it, was an on-ramp on a hill. The woods spread up around the highway and helped to cool the air. There was already an eighteen-wheeler parked along the breakdown lane and another came up behind. I looked in, the drivers were either busy or sleeping and if they had a "no passengers rider" they would likely be of no help. Time passed I knew now I was not far from Flag and Benny Boy. An unfocused pickup truck pulled up and I hopped in the back. I thought that the driver was passing Flag and banged on his roof so he would get off at the exit. As he stopped at the light, I saw if he wanted a few loosies. He was not interested. There was traffic and two guys were waiting spangin for money and goods. I leaped up over the side of the pickup and started talking to them giving them the cigarettes and a joint I had found in the bed of one of the pickups from earlier in the day. They were pumped, to say the least, called me family in Rainbow Gathering terms and I said I had not been to one but was traveling about a month ago with guys who headed to the Gathering in Oregon. There was a bike lying on the ground nearby and they offered it up. As they headed their way in good cheer they pointed the way to ride into town. Now in the same mood hair streaming back, I rolled on into Flagstaff.

The Rainbow attitude and gifting reminded me a bit of Burning Man in Black Rock City, Nevada. For seven days this flat plain of deathly desert known as the playa located 120 miles from Reno become a haven for all sorts of out-there attendees. It drew from artists to drugees to those preaching alternative lifestyles, as well as those just looking for a fun time and who could afford the ticket price. The gifting and bartering reminded me of the Burn the most when bacon was close to gold in terms of its value. The Rainbow guys made me think what the Burn may have been like in years past when the event happened more organically without so many rules, gates, and when there were not yet over fifty thousand people storming the playa each year. Then I would have been free to set off a flamethrower without so much complaining.

I stopped in at a chichi café and got a lemonade to quench my thirst from a cute twenty-one-year-old barista. Her sister was there sitting doing college work with no one else present. I talked casually to them taking my time reading the local paper off and on and ended up getting the barista's number. The bike was left outside and with no lock and in a matter of hours it was stolen. It was the shortest time I've owned a bike in my life and I laughed at the hilarity of the situation. I was not able to contact my friend Ben and thought he might still be coming back from working the Grand Canyon. The good spot to crash ended up being up the hill and back down across from the hospital where there were trees and pavement going into the depths of the woods. Someone had conveniently cut a human-sized hole in the fence to get through. The stars showed through once again as the tall trees cast shadows from the street lamps.

Tip: The barter system works well among travelers. Somebody needs a lighter you may get a cigarette back. Even if you don't smoke you may be able to trade or gift what you've got. If you have something that is valuable to you, use this system judiciously, of course. But you never know. I gave some guys a joint and I got a bicycle back.

Chapter 13

Next day contact was made with Ben.

"Hey, man, am I good to come over?"

Ben said, "Yeah, I got in last night. I just gotta check with roommates. How many days do you think you're stayin?"

I said, "I don't know a few days to a couple weeks."

Ben said, "Well I'll just have to let them know when you get here."

I said, "Well am I good to come over now?"

Ben said slowly, "Sure." And although it was somewhat unclear whether it was OK with the roommates I had the couch for the next few days. He and one of his roommates would knock comments back and forth with each other. Potential flirtation with the younger woman, but not enough for either one of them to admit as roommates, and anyway she was definitely one for attention and a bit of drama. Overall, he was happier than he had been in Prescott while going to college, but his semi-depressed state was still evident. Working in the Grand Canyon for tourists was obviously intense. He definitely had a home to come back to now, but working this kind of intense job the question was when you go away for days or weeks at a time, what do you have to come back to? He was pleased to see me. I was East Coast Jewish as well, darker sense of humor and had known him for a lil while and was a loner as well from time to time. He had people he got along with in Flag, but I don't know if anyone really got to an extent, where he was coming from. On the other hand, when he did get back home, he had his projects of getting a van situated for traveling, climbing, and his drums. While there he and I chipped away at what was left of the tint on the window. Showing me pictures at the same time, Ben said, "I'm going to convert my van so that I'll have space for my climbing rack, a bed to sleep in, and it will all fold up for when I'm driving around."

He had friends, some from work, who he would go climbing with around Flag. He would also bang on his drums letting out frustration. Who knows how true it was when the younger housemate said Ben would laze around for two weeks straight when he had time off. He knew this I'm sure from experience and how much of it was chemical I'm not sure, but I wondered and made it known that some of the depression and frustration may have been due to him simply not pushing himself out of his own comfort zone?

In my time there we went out to the welcoming bars of town. Met two college students when we were sipping on Irish coffees. They were interested in the drink, the brunette asked what it was and we were distracted by conversation snacking on the free popcorn. We started talking and headed out to the deck. The view is the best in terms of the center of town. The bar is on the second floor with a restaurant occupying the first floor and hotel rooms intermingled in back. The whole place is western historical.

Ben was clearly interested in the more aware brunette. I played along though I had no interest in the out-there hippie, not-so-bright friend who would say harmless things, inane things, and then have trouble speaking. Together we hit another night spot with a live band. The girls liked to dance and I did too, but my lack of interest showed through. I may have seen Ben dance before, but in general he didn't like to, and this was a regular night so he just sat and drank his drink. The girls drifted off and he may have got a number, but I don't think either one of us cared too much. While there at least I got Ben out and about talking to some different people, much of this was drinking related. There were more conversations about where we were at in our lives, realities apparent and wanderlust a usual topic. Women on the mind as well.

Even went in with him to see the barista, but nothing doing except some texting later on.

During the day I would go to the library to read and explore the town. Hanging out in the park as I finished lunch there was a local drunk native guy telling me to take his change and looking the worse for wear. Later on, I saw him in the town center and the EMTs rolled up to him saying they had got a call about him. This was not their first meeting. With other ragtag friends and acquaintances around him, he perked up. Seeing this I talked to them saying, "He's alright."

After speaking to him they left him alone to hang around. Flag come summertime is a town for rovers, ramblers, drifters, and who the actual money is made on, your chintzy tourists. It is also one of the closest major cities of any kind to the Denai Rez, the largest Native American reservation in the country known to most as the Navajo Nation, located smack dab on the four corners.

Meanwhile Ben had shot an email off to see if there were any employment opportunities for me at his work. I initially had planned to stay for a couple weeks to find out. But the living situation with the roommates was not ideal and I had gotten word from my friend Matteo that he was heading through from Prescott on his way back to Santa Fe. Didn't know until the next day that it would be my last day. Ben, Ellie his roommate, and I went out with one or two others for Thai food and yucked it up speaking crass and some true bantering back and forth.

Late morning Matteo rolled on through and the two of us went to eat at one of his favorite breakfast places down the street from Ben's and conveniently across the street from the laundromat. Hugging unabashedly since it had been a while. During our first year at Prescott in the second semester, we had lived together at the puke awful colored pink apartments. During the time many a drunken drama was played out. The first thing about the apartments was that when I moved into the cheap shitty two-bedroom there was a mermaid's hair stuck down the bathroom drain. An entire root system was growing out that had to be removed. Also, a guy had been shot about a month before in the apartment above. After Matteo and his roommate moved into the two-bedroom there was a bit of outstanding rent not handled. This was small potatoes compared to the cast of characters who frequented the apartments. Even with the many parties we had, we were the quiet ones. A nice potentially methed-out lady moved in for a short time. Then Ritchie moved in upstairs. A Chicano guy who was friends with many of the young barrio guys and gals, among them were the Creeksider's Gang. He had clearly been locked up before and was amiable enough to everybody, but had a quick temper. On his shaved head was a sizeable skull tattoo. He was still dealing weed but trying to get his life together. Eventually his very attractive black baby mama moved in with their child. They also got the cutest pit bull pup that I've ever seen. Ritchie could be rough with it at times. There were plenty of pit bulls and a couple of Doberman Rottweilers in the Barrio. Every morning for what seemed like a month he would yell down, "Matteo!" Calling him from his slumber on the living room mattress, Matteo would rise like a zombie to start off the day with a wake and bake.

It's a wonder we stayed sane enough with parties always starting on the spur of the moment. One girl in particular named Jess would tell people to meet at the pink apartments come nighttime, without any of the residents knowing what had started. There were two parties of note. One was the Super Bowl, and although the NFL and statisticians may disagree I still call it National Beat Your Wife Day to bring out its insidious culture. It's a day when all the men whose teams have lost and are especially pissed off from betting and being drunk act out their frustration and aggression. Anyway, the New Orleans Saints won and I was thrilled after living down there for a few months. Word from back home in Cambridge came through. My friend John whose mental state was starting to lose hold on reality causing him more trouble for himself had made off with $500 of his mom's money. He had made it down to New York which may have had to do with his crazy as all hell fifty-year-old girlfriend. He then booked a longer and more expensive ticket to Phoenix. Calling me in New Mexico I scrambled knowing things were not right, but not knowing how messed up his mental track was. I made sure that he got a shuttle on up and he happened to arrive on Super Bowl Sunday. He had not all that distinctive brown hair and blue eyes. Many women would describe him as handsome including my mother, but he rarely knew what to do with the admiration. When he arrived there we were caravanning into whiskey row for Mexican. I hopped in the trunk to fit everybody and his eyes went wide. Drinks splashed around with jubilance.

When we got to the house, music was put on and it turned into a laid-back dance party. Matteo returned, more people came over, and the party got pumping. I stepped outside to talk to my friend Ilana and to take a break from sweating. The party started to get more raucous. Matteo's friend Sam had recently broken up with his girlfriend Amanda. In John, Amanda saw a new guy, good looking and different. When she noticed Sam dancing with Ilana she went into my bedroom with John getting close and kissing him. Sam got closer to Ilana. Amanda saw this and was even more pissed. I headed outside for another breather more sweat pouring down my face. Matteo got pissed off at something and started busting up the front door. I came round and he ran into the bathroom glass smashed. Ilana went to the door. People started to slowly move out.

I yelled, "Party's over! Head on out!" John was nowhere to be seen.

I talked through the bathroom door. Ilana talked quietly to Matteo and she was let in. Tim came right around helping to clear people out and headed to the one quiet room leaving the nonsense to the younger ones. Sam was still standing at the bathroom door drunkenly, moaning for Ilana. My aggravation grew.

I told him, "You can see her tomorrow."

He continued calling out "Ilana, Ilana!"

She was of course inside dealing with Matteo's breakdown. After trying to tell him to lay off a couple more times to no effect I was pissed. I talked to Tim and we stood at the ready.

Gravely now, "Sam, we're both from Massachusetts, now that may not mean something to you, but we're not playin, it's time to go."

Finally, we made him leave with me restraining the urge to knock him the fuck out. Shortly thereafter, Ilana then Matteo came out. He was starting to come around. He was barely cut, surprising given all the glass. Comically he had smashed the mirror by throwing a bar of soap at it. John was still nowhere to be found around the house.

When he did come back from across the street he was very apologetic,

"I'm sorry I'm sorry."

He thought he'd had something to do with the incident.

"Nah man, you were fine everyone else was fucking crazy."

The next day we got out and walked up to the highest point of Thumb Butte close to town and he got to see the other side of things, the beauty and the peace you could find out west. It was sunny and dry on one side with trees on the other side, where it was shaded with snow. A good place to think about life if there ever was one. I was getting calls from my mother (my biological mother) about John, she said his mother was worried. Even without this information, he made the decision to head on back. I threw down the money for the immediate flight agreeing that I would be paid back and he went on his way.

The other incident happened on my 22nd birthday. A party with far fewer people this time. Ritchie and friends E, wobbles, Jared and Ritchie's cousin Mikey O were around as well as my friends and school acquaintances. There was also Matteo's friend and potential romantic interest Cailyn. She had brought her friend from New York who was originally from somewhere in Central America. Long and short he had no papers but had lived in the U.S. most of his life. Everything was fine until those two started to argue. Her friend was getting really drunk and she started to shake him against the back wall of the pink apartment. She was vibrant but much smaller than her drunk friend. Their voices kept growing louder in argument. I had had enough on my birthday and grabbed the adjustable shower pole ready to swing bursting outside. I found nobody but this guy lying in the middle of Lincoln Street. With a groan, I called a few others over and we picked him up and brought him inside. Old school machismo had taken over, Mikey O had thought Cailyn's friend was shaking her. As soon as he interpreted things this way, there was no time for talking. He had knocked the poor dumb drunk guy out. I said I would go with the slowly awakening body and Cailyn to the ER. We got a taxi. It being Arizona and the Central American guy not having papers he gave as little information as possible though they asked away. There may have been a bill, but we got out of there as soon as he was conscious (though bloody still), before any medical staff found out more. It was past three in the morning and my birthday was over.

Those were two of the more extreme events from that era, but seeing Matteo again brought them back clearly. We reminisced with him filling in any gaps in my memory. I got my stuff from Ben's. Ellie was sad to see me go and told me, "At least tell Ben." She cared for him and clearly was worried how my abrupt leaving would affect him.

I said I would tell him, knowing that leaving this way was far from ideal, but thinking as a traveler that in the long run, he would get the larger picture. I threw my stuff in Matteo's car, hugged Ellie goodbye and was glad to be back with a more unpredictable mind.

We drove clear across to New Mexico catching up as we went. Once ya cross the border the land changes and this state that I once imagined to be Mars comes into view. From sand dunes ridden around on by ATVs outside of Albuquerque also known as ABQ to the desert and forest rising up from Santa Fe, it is a memorable place with its greens, tans and bright reds. We stopped to admire our surroundings and smoke a J on the off-ramp. Although it was still hot there, there had been historic levels of rain so greenery sprung to life. We headed on into Santa Fe picking beers up on the way with a woman begging for a drink outside. She jumped in front of the car much to Matteo's dissatisfaction. The drinks were gotten, the car rolled on over to see Matteo's boss, a good-hearted friendly hardworking landscaper. I would find out later when his boss let me work for him for two days that these letting off steam events were par for the course come nighttime. After a hot day laboring in various yards the smoke and drink would flow unabated.

Matteo's boss Zeke discussed the business and who had the biggest houses in the area. Some of the houseowners seemed to create their own problems and we heard family dramas drifting out of the windows. The money that was part of their lives caused greed and paranoia. Zeke was looking to expand his business and he had the mind and the work ethic for it. He liked working outdoors but was qualified to be in an office solving complex problems, coding away. Most of the big money properties were in Los Alamos, where there were some of the highest paying federal government jobs in the land. Some jobs in the nuclear industry rounded out at $500,000 a year. You would find the type of too-smart-for their-own-good owner who was a master of physics, but damn if they knew anything about landscaping. In my own experience, it's not surprising when overeducated people trained in the academy pretend to expand their knowledge base outside of their own expertise on practical, day-to-day life matters. For instance, I knew I was not doing the best job landscaping and rolled with it just fine when I was told I could stay back at Matteo's the next day. The repetitive pickaxe into the dry dirt had just about done me in. I just appreciated the opportunity and two days of pay after months of not having anything coming in besides from helpful people or a rolling silver ball, and slots was definitely one way to throw money into the trash. The two days of work found us turning dirt for an aging, funny eccentric woman named Betty with a wild dog. The second the fence was open the dog darted out to the street and around the neighborhood surprising her more reserved neighbors. For her, this must have been a common occurrence. She eventually got the dog back in behind her fence after taking a drive around.

One of the days in Santa Fe we headed over to hang out with another former Prescott College student, Clay. He was back from Cali where he had been filming an experimental skate and travel video. The video was well done for what it was. We gave him our thoughts over a drink and J. Matteo confided later out of frustration,

"He's just making vacation videos."

"Alright, well where's he getting the money from, to travel around and do the videos?"

"We don't really talk about it 'cause he feels uncomfortable about it."

"O so it's family money?"

"Yeah."

"Well that's fine he's just got to be upfront about it and own it."

"Yeah, but he's uncomfortable with the whole situation."

"Fair enough," I said and left it for the time being.

I found myself reflecting on my own adventure in writing. Although I was traveling on my own money, I wondered whether I was doing the same exact thing... Only answer I came up with, with a dry desert mouth waiting in the car for Matteo, was, 'Not exactly.'

I had time. Time to rest my sore body and mind reading on the couch in the desert countryside. The house was open with few doors aside from the bedrooms and bathroom. Time to read time to think. The journey was ending, this journey at least. I had a ticket back to Boston. Time to talk to Ben over the phone, he sounded better than he was during my stay. He sounded like he was more than making it through the day now.

I reflected on the choices of loneliness or smothering claustrophobic control that can come with connection.

There was also time to simply enjoy the stay. There were still street interactions that took place. Like my first day in Santa

Fe when a friendly guy walked me toward the library. He was a functioning heroin addict that had a whole bunch of outdoor gear stowed around the city. He said, "I'll lead," and we walked and chatted away.

Then we made a quick stop ten yards from the creek where he had stowed another brand-new backpack that he had to exchange, putting it onto his shoulders. He had arrived a few months back and now things were looking up with all the stuff he had acquired. He had a wife and kids, but now in middle age, along with the heroin he said, "I've gotten fed up with that life and I'm better off rambling on my own."

Before I took my leave of him at the library, he pointed with a confident military presence at the water fountain as he sweated in his white bandana with ramshackle swagger.

"That's the coldest water in town." Off to the toilet he went.

The one other guy I saw was hunkered down outside of a shopping mall. I made him up a bagel and cream cheese which I was having for breakfast. He claimed he had been a rescuer on 9-11. Who knows? I had my doubts. Before leaving on this journey I heard this claim was not uncommon among certain people with their own delusions living out on the streets of America. Anyways he said he was trying to get himself shipshape to go see his father who owned land in New Mexico. He hadn't seen his dad in years. He gave me a few dollars to go and get him some cheap liquor which I did. Rationalizing that it was a hell of a lot better for him to have it than to go through the DTs out in the unforgiving burning heat of the day. Funny in a sick sort of way that there's a beer with a pink elephant on it called Delirium Tremens. I left him to his own devices.

Given that Matteo and I had met during college orientation when we went out for a couple of weeks with a whole bunch of fellow students to hike in the blue range, it was fitting that we decided to go up a mountain outside of Santa Fe with his roommate Ben. Matteo had not been getting along with Ben. Ben liked him fine but did not understand his dis-ease. Matteo saw Ben as being sheltered and not open to the fact that he had moved out to the southwest where culture, people, and history were different from back east. He thought Ben lacked emotional intelligence. Matteo saw himself as having what would stereotypically be called a feminine side when it came to emotionality. He has always been a free spirit, artistic and while that serves him well, past history dictates that he could be flaky at times. Ben was more the type for bottling up his emotions and getting on with it.

We hiked up, up, up and away passing other hikers as our breaths grew longer, deeper then more hollow with the gaining elevation. Yeah, it was beautiful up there on the saddle between the peaks. I got a little light-headed but kept drinking water. Ben was not doing as well up over ten thousand feet. The home stretch for the night was ahead and there was a mountain lake to look forward to. Down and back up again legs getting tired. There it was the water, crystal clear as the sun arced downward to the horizon. Matteo and I jumped on in, damn it shocked ya back to life. We camped out, ate, and had a good old time. Each of us took turns with the U-Dig-It spade challenging physics shitting, squatting on the slope. It brought back memories of working for Outward Bound especially since the campsite was busy and it was not the easiest to find a private spot.

Breathing was not the easiest, either, and Ben didn't seem to get any sleep. Matteo, on the other hand, was out as usual. I split the difference. He didn't like it, but after living with him and seeing him wake up at one of his many residences in Prescott, I had dubbed him the Energizer Bunny. His head would hit the floor, pillow, mattress, or whatever was closest and he would be out. Ten seconds before he had been up jumping around. He would wake up like Kane from pro wrestling. Lights would immediately turn on in his eyes and he would be off to the races.

Morning came and we cleaned up camp and started to climb the ridge. About halfway up Ben was having a hard time and needed to take breaks. The altitude was setting in. I told him to drink water and take a minute. Matteo went on relating it to E.I. emotional intelligence,

"It's lack of self-care."

"I know," I said in response.

He was also simply not yet used to this environment. We went onward and reached the saddle once again, seeing the peak high up but not too far away.

I said, "You wanna head up?"

"No, there's not enough time," Matteo said. I told Ben that as soon as we got down a few hundred feet it should get easier and easier to breathe. Matteo continued in the lead, me close behind, Ben a little further behind. We started to descend and the pace grew quicker. We caught up to three attractive women in tight yoga pants booties a showing. Along with the hiking it got our blood flowing. We stopped for some water momentarily, then Matteo leaned over to ask,

"You wanna catch up with them?"

He was off and I was close behind jogging with backpacks bumping down the mountain. We kept going, but where were they? One of the girl's had legs that were pretty long. He didn't catch up with them until they were inside their car parked right next to ours in the parking lot. I was out of breath. Matteo had a few words about seeing them around town, but it was more about the chase. Ben came down a little confused, fine, tired and breathing better. That night we all had beers and a barbecue with Lizzy, Matteo's other roommate and the most responsible one of the house, who came back and joined us. There was still some disagreement between Ben and Matteo, but with beers in hand, a fire going, stars out, and good, home-cooked food, joy and commonality won out for the night.

The night crept into morning and the trip had been a foreshadowing of what was to come for Ben. A dark premonition of an incoming reality. His girlfriend called and wanted to break up. He broke down then acted like there wasn't much wrong. We had all heard his phone conversation, which proved otherwise. He and his girlfriend had been doing the long-distance thing for a while. I always thought that any agreed-upon lack of physical contact based on the principles of monogamy was a bit loco. Especially when you're young you got needs. You're human, I know I am. Ben was broken up about it, but was still hanging on thinking that the situation could be rectified.

Anyway everyone was moving out of the house and neither one of us wanted to hear about relationship problems. Matteo was moving to Santa Fe and for this occasion I decided to help with the move, showing off the red devil, shiny black shoes and all, sweating away for style's sake. It was hot sweaty and the golden zoot suit chain clinked against the objects we moved in. The wild outdoor remote feeling was gone, in its place was convenience and a small house that would be more practical on a day to day basis.

After the move, we went to the local bar and the bartender serving was tall, dark, curvy, and very attractive in a Rosario Dawsonesque way. Matteo knew the staff well from many an imbibed drink. I mentioned what I had been doing for the past months and Nichole the bartender had her own backstory. She traveled up the west coast trying to hitch. But two intense looking darker skinned women had a hard time getting rides. Nichole had been more of a train-hopper and traveler with friends. Arriving in Burlington, Vermont she met a black very Christian woman who was amazed by her. She had kids and a husband back home and had not been with a woman before. Titillated by the young free spirit and her story they hooked up. A few details Nichole recalled mixed with my imagination and I found myself visualizing the woman in conservative clothes coming across the young bawdy traveler. Who was she and why did she look so rough, yet confident and sexy? How was she so free? The conservative woman had a long-repressed gleam in her eye. The traveler gal's attitude allowed her to see that the woman was hesitant but interested. The boundaries between the two built the sexual tension.

"We talked for a time. Summer light grew dim. It happened twice," Nichole confided to me, light flashing from her eyes in the dim bar light.

"The first time, that time, the conservative grew less conservative and I invited her back to the traveling van. Strangely, there was no one in the van for a change. I took her hand firmly and somehow softly at the same time. I could see a spark growing inside Christian, a spark that had not been felt before. I could tell inside she was trembling, but outside she was focused on me as I moved around the van mystically. Christian sat down next to me. I put my hand into her lap."

I imagined as I looked up at Nichole how Christian warmed and how between her legs there was a wetness.

Nichole went on, "I leaned in to steal a kiss. She turned away, but the gleam in her eyes grew bright in the dim light of the van. She leaned back in planting the first kiss on my lips. Ohhhhh I leaned back and smiled."

"'Did I do something wrong?' she said nervously. 'No,' I said leaning back in. 'Do it again this time add a little tongue.' We were swimming in each other's company."

She poured another drink our eyes met and she continued.

"I could see her thinking to herself at first, I'm scared not knowing what I'm doing too, I only want to kiss you, kiss you over and over."

I got a dry mouth hanging on her every word and downed the drink quickly. She turned to the side as she poured yet another for me. Her breast rose in her white tank top as she breathed in lifting the glass to the tap.

"The next time it happened I went to Christian's house and it was later still. Christian had put her kids to sleep and her husband was working out of town. I came to her window stepping on the latticework."

I pictured her black Doc Martens leaving a print of coal on the white paint.

Nichole smiled with mischief as she said, "She opened her window with a start even though she knew I was coming."

"Quietly, please, my kids are asleep."

"I rolled through the window and landed with a thud. She looked around paranoid at the noise. Not a child had stirred.

'Sorry, sorry,' I half apologized looking into her eyes. All the fear that she had felt slipped away. We stepped towards each other's bodies coming together in a heated embrace. Breasts quivering nipples becoming erect."

A light came to her eyes as she flashed her teeth. My imagination ran, conjuring bodies both ample and curvaceous.

Nichole continued, "My dirty short hair rubbed against the side of her long, straightened hair. My teeth brushed her neck. Down I went moving to her breasts licking as I went. Down further still hands sliding along her nightgown. My hands firmly on her ankles. My hands quickly now moving up her inner thighs. Christian said, 'I'm so wet, wetter then anytime with my husband.'

"My fingers slid inside. Tension increased at the moment another moment tension built inside. Then it stopped. I removed my hand, she opened her eyes and instinctively sat down on the bed wondering if something was wrong. Then just as she was about to look down I felt her tense it was the smallest licking like a cat. Her hand grasped my hair as I went down. The tension was back ebbing and flowing continuing to build with small circles I made with my tongue. Her back arched.

"'What was this?' Christian must have wondered," as I stared into my glass, my own blood heated by the warmth of this sexy tale.

"The circles grew more intense. Her hips flinched. Flickering, flickering still. Then finally exaltation breathing heavily legs back askew.

"I nuzzled up on the bed laying my head on her chest resting there. Her hips flinched ever so slightly as they spooned in comfort fitting snugly into my pelvis. We talked softly and she confided, 'You know it's the first time I've orgasmed in my whole life.'

"The first time she had gotten the release?! After an hour I watched as her eyes began to dim toward sleep. I got up and slipped out the window."

I would picture it from another barstool years after and thousands of miles away. It was Oh so clear. Christian rose looking out, and all she could see was Nichole's messy short hair receding into the distance.

Her story raised my temperature and I was intrigued. Now she had kids of her own at home from a man she was no longer with. Long gone were the days of the dykey rough n tumble traveler. Now she had shorter hair that hung to the side very feminine in tight jeans and tank top breasts playfully pushed together, a smile coming across her mouth flash of teeth, smooth lips and playful eyes to make ya keep attention. We kept talking she kept pouring um up. Lack of transport running in the mind. Even if it wouldn't work I should have invited her back. The memory still tickles the imagination. And of course not only the mind. Bid farewell.

Still, to this day, there's this underlying desire, longing for a deeper connection. Longing for more. That more is possibly meeting someone traveling you never knew existed, meeting eyes in Vermont, crossing paths outside Portland. Sharing that sense of longing across a bar. That longing not just of someone, but of the rarely known and unknown that you have set out for. A longing for the concrete and the ethereal.

In the end, I had both freed myself and become more stuck. I freed myself with a jump into the back of that pickup truck in Needles. I rode out of Needles hair cascading back in the wind Arizona in view and the Mojave left behind. I rode into Flagstaff on the bike with worries cast asunder. Energy within and all possibilities in view. In this second part of the journey, I had become more stuck in both new and old relationships, with family and friends, from romantic to purely sexual encounters. My fortunes changed romantically, but ended up back in the same pattern of coming together then quickly falling apart. With close friends, I followed an old pattern, too, though one that was more stable than the romances. One of reaffirmation and strengthening the bonds between us. I had a brief view into each one of their lives. My momentum and intensity probably assigned more meaning to the individual moments than there was cause for. My relation with family was stable even if their lives were in flux. They were there even if our views on each other tended to remain static. A shared history and familial roles can do this to two people no matter if both of you have actually changed greatly. So at times the momentum stayed the same from the first part of the journey, but what really changed once I was in the West was the deepening of relationships to people around me. I met my goal of reaching the Pacific and I had also managed to reestablish some relationships. Fulfillment though comes from within and is usually temporary.

And then what? Once the goals have been met? What then? Life goes on... To what end?

I was heading back east on the roadrunner train from Santa Fe to Albuquerque. Back to the Boston area back to family and longtime friends. What for? Well, money was running low and the first part of the trip needed typing up. Ahh, but what for really? Matteo made me think. I commonly counter to other people that we should all stop thinking in black and white when it comes to reflecting on things and living your life in general. I tend to see in shades of grey. But it is harder, much harder still, to see in color. Seeing in color is taking the world in all its vibrancy, mundaneness, largess, minimalism, from multiple points of view and from different realities, physical, mental, and even metaphysical, and to try to do this all at the same time. It is no easy task. I only saw glimpses here and there along the way when in a state of flow, those times when you are consumed by one moment. In that one moment, you catch everything that your mind can take in.

Try to see in color,
Until next time somewhere in the world.

-Alex Silberman

Glossary

Decline of Western Civilization: Part I: The Los Angeles punk music scene circa 1980 is the focus of this film. *Part II: The Metal Years. Part III: The Decline of Western Civilization III* is a 1998 documentary film that follows the gutter punk lifestyle of homeless teenagers. -IMDB

Festy Kid: A young person who enjoys serially going to festivals with drugs usually following shortly behind.

Gas Chugging: Obtaining gas by asking patrons of gas stations to squirt into the container you are holding.

Johnny Hobo: A well-known folk punk singer among travelers. Also known as Pat the Bunny.

Mickey D's: McDonalds

OG: Original gangsta

Rainbow Gathering: Rainbow Gatherings are temporary intentional communities, [1] held annually in various locations in the United States, Canada, Mexico, Russia, and Europe. These gatherings seek to encourage the practice of ideals of peace, love, respect, harmony, freedom and community, and seek to serve as an alternative to consumerism, capitalism, and mass media. They are strongly associated with counterculture and the hippie subculture. https://en.wikipedia.org/wiki/Rainbow_Gathering

Rez: Slang for Indian Reservation

SAC: Sacramento, California

Spanging: Begging for spare change

CPSIA information can be obtained
at www.ICGtesting.com
Printed in the USA
FSHW012334040220
66652FS